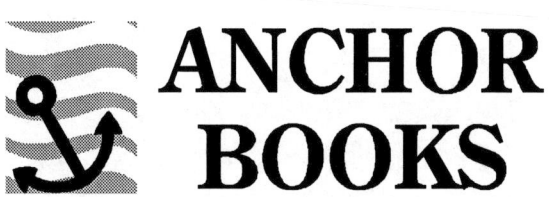

ANCHOR BOOKS

A GIFT OF NATURE

Edited by

Steph Park-Pirie

First published in Great Britain in 2004 by
ANCHOR BOOKS
Remus House,
Coltsfoot Drive,
Peterborough, PE2 9JX
Telephone (01733) 898102

All Rights Reserved

Copyright Contributors 2003

SB ISBN 1 84418 297 5

FOREWORD

Anchor Books is a small press, established in 1992, with the aim of promoting readable poetry to as wide an audience as possible.

We hope to establish an outlet for writers of poetry who may have struggled to see their work in print.

The poems presented here have been selected from many entries, and as always editing proved to be a difficult task.

I trust this selection will delight and please the authors and all those who enjoy reading poetry.

Steph Park-Pirie
Editor

CONTENTS

Inspiration?	Helen Trevatt	1
Walking On An Autumn Day	Roland Seager	2
Acorn Tree	Carol Mary Woods	3
Nature At Its Best	Evelyn M Harding	4
Favourite Places	Dulcie George	5
Trees	Linda Cooper	6
A Breath Of Fresh Air	Olliver Charles	7
The Mouse	Brian Bateman	8
Rose	Christopher W Wolfe	9
Roses	P J Cain	10
October Dawn	Jonathan Pegg	11
Our Friends Around Us	Barbara Jermyn	12
The Lake District	Margaret Goodfellow	13
Summer Sunset	Lorraine Noble	14
My Tree	Sylvia Fox	16
Sunset Sky	John Wilson Smith	17
A Day Out	Denise Seymour	18
The Thunderstorm	Eileen Cuddy Buckley	19
The Dance Of The Swallows	Ruth Dewhirst	20
Hunter's Moon	Robert E Fraser	21
Parknight	W Ashwell	22
Heaven	D A Robertson	23
Nature's Spell	Leo Taylor	24
Inspired By Nature	Vanessa Jane Haynes	25
I Planted A Tree	Alex Anderson	26
The Sky At Night	Rachael Ford	27
Summertime	Lil Bordessa	28
Nature's Little Things	Margaret B Baguley	29
Autumn Red	T I R	30
Spring	M C Barnes	32
Childhood Playground	Anne Eves	33
Rain	Paul Birkitt	34
Daffodils	Diana Mudd	35
The Coming Of Spring	Tracey Lynn Birchall	36
Walking Hot	Michael D Bedford	37
The Flames Of Autumn	Jean McGovern	38

Autumn	Clare Todd	39
Unstaged Perfection	C D Goldsmith	40
The Swan	Janet Brook	41
A Quandary	Bryan Park	42
Summer	John Mitchell	43
June	Mary Long	44
Beware The Male	Kim Montia	45
Beauty's Bright	A A Murphy	46
Garden Dreams	Beryl Smyter	47
Oh! Ponder As You Pass Through	Sheila Johnson	48
A Spring Drive Near Broughton, Northants	Paul Wilkins	49
Below An English Tree	M J Banasko	50
Summer And Fall	William A Mack	51
Secret Garden	Carole Morris	52
A Little Escape	Geraldine McMullan Doherty	53
The Day	Libi Garner	54
Creations Of Nature	Margery Rayson	55
Colours In Bloom	Imelda Fitzsimons	56
Late Autumn	Sammy Michael Davis	57
Yesterday's News	Rebecca Gurney	58
By The Shore	William H Precey	59
Nature's Garden	Anthony Walton	60
Nature At Its Best	Margaret Marston	61
A Day In The Life Of A Tree	Sue Elle	62
Healing Calmness	Anne Gray	64
Beauty Of The Countryside	Glenys Moses	66
Dreaming Of The Dales	Jack Ellison	67
The Pale Moon Rises	Julia Pegg	68
High Summer	Lyn Hunter	69
Thank You	Sharon Grimer	70
Ramblers' Rap	John Belcher	71
English Countryside	Jill Lowe	72
The World Is Such A Lovely Place	Christine Corby	73
Summer Morn	J Hewing	74
Inspired By Nature	Ena Field	75
Night	Dot Holloway	76

Beauty Of The Beach	Clare M Ashton	77
And Autumn Approaches	Dan Pugh	78
The Tree Of Life	Norman Meadows	80
Capricious Autumn	Celia G Thomas	81
Killarney	Jo Robinson	82
Enchanted Wood	Marilyn Davidson	83
Fleet Of Foot	Anita Richards	84
It Is Winter	Richard Stead	85
In Sweet Violets	Hardeep Singh-Ledder	86
A Summer Place	Elizabeth Hiddleston	87
Mother Nature	Grace Harding	88
Delightful	Harry Crompton-Fils	89
Last Breath Of Summer	Elizabeth Amy Johns	90
Mother Nature Returns	Sallie Chilcott	91
Mountains	Alan Wilson	92
Summer Haze	Angy Lindsay	93
October	Sheila J Leheup	94
Creation	J Allen	95
Nature	Iris Davey	96
Colours	Joanne G Castle	97
The Happy Valley	S H Smith	98
My Garden	Hazell Dennison	99
Autumn Is Not The End	Kathy Rawstron	100
Home Sweet Home	Julia Amos	101
In Bluebells	Nick Hall	102
Summer Storm	Jillian Mounter	103
The Worker	Patricia Whittle	104
Be Still My Heart	Lyn Sandford	105
Happy Memories	Stella Bush-Payne	106
The Season Of Change	Sheila Storr	107
Butterfly Ridge	Ernest Hannam	108
A Leaf	Ted Gutridge	110
Spring	Margaret Browne	111
September Splendour	Betty McIlroy	112
Devon Spring	Edward Fursdon	113
Spring	Joan D Bailey	114
An October Day	Doreen Petherick Cox	115
Come And Find Me	Lorna Lea	116

Cobwebs And Sunlight	R K Bowhill	117
Nature's Weatherlore	David A Garside	118
Seascape	Doreen F Jackson	119
Nom De Fleurs	Roger Mosedale	120
Thoughts Of Yesterday	Meg Claybrook	121
Nature's Embrace	Wynn Stone	122
The Red Kites	Laura P Williams	123
Take The Time	Mary Neill	124
Cycling In Turkey	Charmain Goldwyn	126
Norman's Tree	Maureen Tooze	127
Autumn	Betty Hattersley	128
A Forest Walk	Jennifer Collins	129
Mister Whisty Cloud	Eric Ferris	130
October In The Garden	June Melbourn	131
Rain, Rain, Rain	J A Easterlow	132
Autumn Dawn	Stuart Wood	133
The Maiden Spring	Joy Saunders	134
The Day Shift	I R Finch	135
Butterflies	Fran Vincent	136
Ode To Nature	Rosemary Davies	137
The Peace Of The Snow	Fay Smith	138
Almost Entirely Uninspired	Ross Harrison	139
Keep Looking Up	Elma Heath	140
Autumn	Dan Del'ouest	141
On Top Of The Downs	Steve Darlow	142
Country Peace	Edith Buckeridge	143
Rain	Jenny Stevens	144
The Countryside	Joan Magennis	145
Gentle Rain	Kathleen M Hatton	146
Storm	E Balmain	147
The Sun Worshipper	E D Bowen	148
Vibgyor	Maureen Westwood O'Hara	149
Bright Prospect	Gareth Wynne Richards	150
Pond Life	Brian Strand	151
Hedgerows In June	Reg James	152
The Wilderness	Ruth Morris	153
The Colours Of Springtime	John Harrison	154
Blooming Lovely	Winsome Mary Payter	155

Memories Of Life	E M Eagle	156
Hope	F R Smith	157
Four Seasons	Rachel Mary Mills	158
Transformation	Tricia Sturgeon	159
Colourful Sky	Ethel Wakeford	160
The Rose	Rozetta Pate	161
Drum Rolls In The Park	B Wardle	162
A Hidden Flower	Rebecca Timothy	163
Secrets Of The Forest	Marjorie Leyshon	164
The Nest	Christine Spall	166
Nature's Bounty	Margaret Parnell	167
Summer Senses	G D Furse	168
Frog Bog - Cool Pool	Barbara Thomas	170
Spare A Thought	Wendy Meeke-Davies	171
Rainbows Of Cheer	Joan Egre	172
Butterflies	Terry Daley	173
Changes	Christine Gibson	174
Vallee de Mai	Sudha Shrotria	175
The Seasons	Jilly Tynan	176
Summer	Lydia Barnett	177
Way Of The River	Anthony Grimes	178
Global Destruction	D Richards	179
Our Planet Earth	D Adams	180
A Springtime Flower	Mrinalini Dey	181
Fluoxotine Dream	Dawn Gillespie	182
Summer's Eve	Les Davey	183
The Autumn Of Me	Ian Fisher	184

INSPIRATION?

You wear your colours so bright and new,
You startle the birds, up in the sky so blue.
A little shooting bud is beginning to show,
Over the next few weeks you will continue to grow.

There is kindness in your smile as you open up to the sun,
Your beauty will inspire, many hearts will be won.
You are fully grown, such a sight we do behold,
For you are a newly bloomed rose, the colour of gold.

You have spread your spores; your children will be fed,
To enhance my garden you share my flowery bed.
I pick each bloom with care and undying love,
May you carry on your lineage with light from above.

Winter is here now and you are fast asleep,
I know you're aware but your secrets you do keep.
I will tend you, feed you till the spring does appear,
And I know we will enjoy another glorious year.

Helen Trevatt

WALKING ON AN AUTUMN DAY

As the winter time draws near
A different scene will I find here
Gentle falls the leaves as yet
But soon a storm will they beget
Only the evergreens to cling
Soon fewer songbirds here to sing
Then fallen leaves a carpet weave
A different beauty to achieve
With frost upon the grass to glow
And if there's snow, what a delight
Beneath the yellow moon at night

Roland Seager

ACORN TREE

As I look outside the window
there I see a beautiful acorn tree
blowing wildly as can be, blowing free
with its long, swaying branches like arms
that can cradle all your charms
with its little brown acorns blowing in the wind
and the sound of its crackling, whistling, homely leaves
that shelter in the rain,
I love to watch the acorn tree again and again.

Carol Mary Woods

NATURE AT ITS BEST

Nature brings us a mind full of things,
Newborn lambs a-leaping in the spring,
The smell of fresh mown grass
Telling us that winter now has passed.

Looking forward to the summer sun,
Lazing about in it and having fun.
Conjuring up a sandy beach,
The lapping waves just in reach.

Little white clouds a-floating by,
Birds singing merrily in the sky.
What a feeling it gives to me,
Nature's generous gifts offered and free.

Autumn with the leaves of red and gold,
Dropping from the trees, a sight to behold.
Then comes the winter snow, a different scene,
Showing up the robin's breast, as he comes to feed.

Evelyn M Harding

FAVOURITE PLACES

Many are the places I have been
Many are the wonders I have seen
From English wood to Scottish moor
From riverbank to seaside shore

In the woodlands I recall
Primroses and violets small
Anemones like stars above
Two young people much in love

On the moorland one may see
Purple heather, a grouse maybe
And overhead the seagulls cry
Making for a loch nearby

Near the riverbank is seen
A kingfisher, a flash of green
Reflections of the evening sky
As an almost silent skiff glides by

But there's nowhere like the rolling sea
Where the wind blows fresh and the birds fly free
A distant ship and a sandy shore
No one, with grace, could ask for more.

Dulcie George

TREES

I open my door and I see them
Magnificent trees towering high
English elms, that stand proudly before me
Their foliage obliterating sky.

Green fluttering leaves through the summer
Russet gowns, when the green mantle's gone,
Swirling dead leaves on the pavement
Warmed by the late autumn sun.

Stark and bare when the winter wind blows them
Breaking the force of the gale,
Seeing the rain lash the branches
And the onslaught of winter hail.

I stand and observe all their beauty
When the trees are covered with snow
I'm enthralled by the transfiguration
And it sets my heart aglow.

The splendour of elms in the sunshine
Their strength when skies are grey
Gives me, pleasure unending
And they're the start of every day.

Linda Cooper

A Breath Of Fresh Air

A breath of fresh air in the
garden - seeing things in the
cold light of day. Plants pay their
rent to stay in the picture,
with fruit and blooms throughout the
year. Young shoots sit up, expecting
praise for doing nothing at
all - just attention seeking.

Birds snatch berries almost before
they have had time to ripen -
like children snatching teacakes
before they have had time to cool.

Briefly pampering the shrubs
with secateurs, like a
hairdresser applying the
final snips to stylish hair.

And those darling rainbow-like
flowers, oh how they attract
attention to themselves -
flirting in the breeze, hoping
I'd notice them. It is like
looking through a kaleidoscope -
seeing one thousand nine hundred
and twenty-nine purple rose
petals dancing in the breeze. A
breath of fresh air in the garden.

Olliver Charles

THE MOUSE

If I had wings and could fly away,
You would be sad and wish I'd stay.
If I had a bushy tail and lived in a tree,
You would leave out food and look for me.

But I have no wings or a bushy tail,
I don't make my bed in a tree,
Oh why are you filled with fear,
When you see me?

A hole is where I make my bed,
For I am just a mouse,
And you wish me dead.

I have no red upon my breast,
No fancy colours on my side,
I am a mouse and I have to hide.

Squirrels come and go, birds fly away,
I am a mouse and I'm here to stay.
Food you leave is a deadly cocktail,
Just look for me, I will not fail.

When you put out food for me,
Feel a little sympathy,
I am just a creature that has to hide.
The red on my lip and the pain in my side.

Squirrels come and go, birds fly away,
I am a mouse,
And I'm here to stay!

Brian Bateman

Rose

Let she of talling elegance display,
Her tender rose, as vivid scarlet hue,
When mood will bathe beneath of yellow ray,
And charm will beauty 'pon the heavens' blue;
Of petal fold, her breath and fragrance sound,
To subtle blend upon the passive beam,
Where slender phrase and innocence abound,
Silent, with endless fringe of summer seam;
As cultivated leaf of meeted wing,
Do sleek her stem and teeth so finely tuned,
Within the soul, may bless and wonder bring,
To glaze, where skirt surround her neatly bloomed;
So proud are forefathers brood and breed,
Befall to lovers' hearts when lovers need.

Christopher W Wolfe

ROSES

Roses exude their fragrant perfume,
Dressed in a gown of velvet maroon,
Beaded raindrops like crystals suspend
Adorning each petal they shimmer and blend.
No artist could capture the beauty I see
Created by God especially for me.

P J Cain

OCTOBER DAWN

A plane's vapour trail, slashes across the morning sky.
Glowing in the rising sun like a mighty comet's tail.
'Tis mid October and the burnished and burning trees,
Stir in the rising breeze, shaking their skirts seductively
As if they are gypsy dancers, bent on merriment.
Enticing their male partners to join them in play.
Such fine regalia bought in some Eastern bizarre,
Full of such fleeting promise,
Which will be cast before the month is over,
To be thrown down like Cleopatra's carpet
Quickly ruined by the chill autumnal rains,
As if dashed by the might of ancient Rome.
The serpent asp becomes the worm which turns.
The dawn mist has finally lifted.
The sun disintegrating her fine and flimsy gown.
The air is yet damp and chill,
Bears no ill will to the slight morning frost
Whilst the sky above me glows an azure blue
And the year though dying, seems wonderful
Having been washed by last night's drop of rain.
How, in all that is holy could I of this morn complain?
Autumn tears now drying in this great dying time.
Such a fitting grande finale; a golden gala
On this most fleeting of passing seasons.
Come next month, these lush trees will be nude.
Ready to be abused by all that winter brings.
Stripped down to the barest of bones,
Whether they be in stands or stand alone,
Giving the winter skyline, a stark yet special appeal.
Horizon fingered silhouettes, as sol's fiery globe sets.

Jonathan Pegg

OUR FRIENDS AROUND US

Using senses, gestures, odours and body stances,
Squawking, squeaking, chirping and foot tapping dances
Animals of the world talk, play, flirt and woo,
To win their mates, it's a pantomime true.

Skunks of the world send out an odour,
Like a chemical bullet to choke an invader,
Is it fear or is it just plain fun,
When he sees his invader on the run?

Birds of the world are imitators, you'll recall,
Producing sounds of a rhythmic self-made musical,
They tease and flirt and even show their red vest,
To get a mate, to share its nest.

Fish of the oceans deep, communicate,
They cluk, bark, click and snap at such a rate,
With an encore of scrape and rasp if trouble's near
And chit-chat to attract the ladies dear.

Fireflies of this world are experts at Morse code,
With three flashes a second apart, they're very bold,
A complicated flash for a potential mate,
Flashes at intervals could mean do not be late.

Male wolf spiders of this world lure their mate,
Its their hairy legs, she says, that makes them great,
Please don't wax, is the message she sends out
And I will woo you have no doubt.

Looking at these living creatures,
Aren't we in awe of their features,
They give glory to the Creator of the all,
We give Him thanks, and we stands tall.

Barbara Jermyn

The Lake District

Sweet smelling flora, pastures green
Sweep upward towards this awesome scene
Peaks and troughs are standing proud
Clouds hang low in pure white shrouds.

Red sails billow in the breeze
Man stands proud, surveys the scene
Babbling waters, rippling stones
A transformation to expose.

A white stone cottage completes the view
Its grey slate tiles take on the hue
Smoke curls up towards the sky,
Circling round those ridges high.

Rowan, beech and mountain ash
Clinging onto hillside crags
This is the Lake District in all its grandeur
A precious jewel of magnificent splendour.

Margaret Goodfellow

SUMMER SUNSET

At that confusing time of day
Shifting suddenly between dark and fair,
She makes her startling entrance
Slyly catching watchers almost unaware.

No prior warning does she provide
Nor distinct sight or crashing sound,
She travels unexpectedly,
Creeping belly lagging on the flattened ground.

Transforming leafy trees from bright emerald
To heavy shades of green,
Warning all primitive life
To scatter safely to their secluded beds unseen

Diminishing sunbeams begin a moving display
Of her lethargic pirouettes,
Cunningly perverting architectural features
To barely distant silhouettes.

Amber lights follow each other keenly
Across the rapidly fading screen,
Hurry all who anticipate the mighty spectacle
As now she's nearly seen.

As nature's indignation prepares her answer
To Heaven's impressive glow,
One last relentless chance to stand meekly
Before her dazzling fiery show.

That was her final great opportunity
To dominate, display and rejoice,
Mere mortals can't expect to reproduce
Such a passionately scenic voice.

Finally disguised in her ghoulish cloak
She attempts her demise to fake,
Gloomy despair her replacement
As romance is dispersed until we wake.

Tonight she rests and gathers strength
To generate another show in place,
Tomorrow perhaps if all is well
She'll come again to represent her grace.

Lorraine Noble

MY TREE

There she stood - tall and stately,
Etched against the frost-blue skies,
Adorned with nature's diamonds,
Her beauty pleased my eyes.

But when the sky was leaden grey,
Her branches soaked and dripping tears,
She seemed to threaten, as I passed -
My childish heart soon filled with fears.

Then one day a gleam of sun,
Would give my tree this glorious sheen,
And I would see her lovely limbs,
Were clothed in palest shimmering green.

As summer came her beauty grew,
I sat beneath the shade she spread.
Unseen I climbed amidst her branches,
Long forgotten, all my dread.

My tree excelled herself in autumn,
She dressed in russet, red and gold.
Look at me, she seemed to cry,
Oh! How I loved this tree so bold.

All too soon she shed her leaves,
Ankle deep around they lay.
Children kicked and shuffled through,
On their way to school each day.

The seasons turned full circle,
Many years have sped along,
But there she stands - my lovely tree,
Stately - tall - and still so strong.

Sylvia Fox

Sunset Sky

When all the daily tasks are done,
I trace the pathway of the sun
As slowly to the west he goes
Majestic as the hour he rose.

Torn ribboned cloud stretched from the west
Reflect his form in colours dressed,
An ever changing patterned sky
Is magic to the questing eye,

Creating forms of fairy land
That come and go on either hand,
With castles that are built on air,
Through columns of the night wind there.

Then forming mountains vast and high
Whose transient shapes fill half the sky
With rose red peaks of ice and snow
To crown the valley here below,

Whilst round my feet the shadows creep
And wander up the village street
To lose themselves in twilight's gloom
That tell me night is coming soon.

The sunsets are not mine alone,
For these rich treasures all may own.
Just stand and gaze at sunset sky,
Let not this beauty pass us by.

John Wilson Smith

A Day Out

Walking through the woods, the other day,
We looked at all the trees along the way,
An enormous oak stood with its branches swaying
And quite close by a bushy squirrel was playing,
Just one glimpse, that's all we got
Then back into the tree he shot.

On we walked, and on, and on
And through the trees the sun shone,
The twigs were snapping as we walked
And to our right a bird squawked,
A little swallow, flying by
And look! A magpie way up high.

How lovely to be in the woods today;
To see nature at its best display,
A little stream trickling by
And now it's time to climb over the sty,
Soon to the park, we will arrive
And onto the roundabouts the children will dive.

Hurrah, hurrah, we're here at last
Onto the swings faster than fast,
Then down to the pond and throw in the bait
Then it was wait and wait and wait.
At last a pike the worm it took
Wriggling and writhing at the end of the hook.

Then it was time to say goodbye,
Back down the path and over the sty.
The sycamores shuddered as the wind blew,
The grass was still wet with the morning dew.
The silver birch and the beech so tall
Seemed to be waving goodbye to us all.

Denise Seymour

THE THUNDERSTORM

It came early in the morning, just as it was growing light,
Murmuring in the distance, after a long and sultry night.
It grew in intensity, then dark yellow was the sky,
Slight rumblings in the distance warned a thunderstorm was nigh.
Then crashing and banging, so loud now the sound,
Roaring, lightning flashing, rain lashing the ground.
Glorious, magnificent, nature at its scary best,
This thunderstorm raged across the sky, fulfilling its quest.
The storm reached a crescendo, just like a symphony,
Then gradually it started to fade away, still in harmony.
By degrees the dark gloom lifted, and light spread around,
Thunder now in the distance, and so faint the sound.
And it was a reminder, how wondrous nature can be,
Never ever take it for granted, in its pure majesty.

Eileen Cuddy Buckley

THE DANCE OF THE SWALLOWS

Dancing, dancing, there up in the air,
Twirling swiftly around without a care,
For this is the dance of the swallows,
And each one their chosen leader follows.

The sun is shining, and the sky is blue,
The green grass is wet with the morning dew,
Up there above us the swallows fly,
Twirling and dancing 'neath the azure sky.

Dancing, dancing, there up in the air,
Twirling swiftly around without a care,
For this is the dance of little swifts,
Flying so high up there above the cliffs.

The noonday sun shines high in the sky,
As on and up towards the clouds they fly,
Twirling and dancing in joyful glee,
Far below is the stormy green-blue sea.

Dancing, dancing, there up in the air,
Twirling swiftly around without a care,
For this is the dance of the seagulls,
As they follow so close to the ships' hulls.

In the evening the red sun has set,
The fishermen have let down their net,
When the bright sun rises up in the east,
Birds are freer by far than man or beast.

Ruth Dewhirst

HUNTER'S MOON

Beware, when barn owl's screeching cry
As the hunter's moon like an orange eye
Hangs, a lantern in the autumn sky
Lighting reynard's prowl

Along the hedgerow, through the field
Where stubble shows the harvest yield
A stealthy shadow, half concealed
Menacing fur and fowl.

The rabbits in their burrow hide
A tiny vole takes a water slide
As a deathly hush garbs the countryside
Marking reynard's prowl.

By the river's tree-lined brink
Where daytime sad-eyed cattle drink
See the red-eyed hunter slink
On his nightly prowl.

Robert E Fraser

PARKNIGHT

By large locked gates you slip
unhindered through easeful space,
leaving the busy road behind.
Segmented car lights race
Slantingly through,
groping damply for elusive you,
but you slide into
the not-quite-dark
of an altogether different
North London park.

Dogs dodge skittishly about,
unsure of shadows, trees,
unfamiliar scents.
Through gracious glass
elongated lights
tinge sleeping grass
a ghostly hue.
The path - a still, choked stream -
gleams ahead of you.
Distant coots bleakly call
across the pale lake.

A severed bough of windswept oak
reclines - a giant's limb,
huge craggy knee
reflecting white in
milk moonlight.

All this you see.

W Ashwell

HEAVEN

I found Heaven in my garden.
Just sitting there quietly one day.
It's just a feeling of peace and contentment
That doesn't seem to come very often everyone's way.
I didn't have to dig to find it,
Or even have to pay
I just sat there very contented
And watched the birds at play.

The sun was shining brightly
So very hot I'll soon have to move and go away.
But I feel I should write down this feeling
I feel this summer's day.
How can I explain these flowers
Only planted in May?
So colourful and in so much abundance
I simply like looking at them each day.
If only I could share it with you
That's all I like to say
The breeze is gently blowing
The leaves on the trees rustling,
Adding to the magic in my garden
This lovely summer's day.

So that's how I found Heaven in my garden
It's not too far away
But it's very hot,
Time has come to move away.

D A Robertson

NATURE'S SPELL

If only you were quiet and closed your eyes
And lay down very softly in a wood
It's possible the trees would send you thoughts
That you'd dismiss as thinking people should.

Then you might sense the calm and fall asleep,
Surrender to some magic as you lay
And capture something strange you can't explain,
But the spell that's cast will haunt you through the day,
And your 'normal' world won't seem the same again.

Leo Taylor

INSPIRED BY NATURE

Bulrushes rise above the earth
Gallantly breezing, within the turf
Buttercups prettily stand in their view
Gazing as I look across, thinking of you

Dandelions and daisies, in the meadow lea
Cows are a-grazing, watching over me
All the wild in their turn
Look out upon the river fern

People taking in their stride
A gentle walk, where they may hide
Our amongst the green grass bank
Watching where some boats had sank

Sunshine bright in summer's view
A tiny bird with a tinge of blue
Whistling softly in a tree
Pleasantly chirping up at me

Grasshoppers jumping, here and there
Silences reigning beyond compare
Butterflies swiftly in full flight
Others unaware of nature's plight.

Vanessa Jane Haynes

I Planted A Tree

I planted a tree
    in my garden,
and summer long it grew.

And in its branches
    settled birds
in all their feathers blue.

They sang for me
    a dainty song
the winds of summer knew.

And was that not
    a kindly thing
for little birds to do?

Alex Anderson

THE SKY AT NIGHT

When the day is at an end
and daylight passes by
sunset falls upon the land
as bright colours fill the sky.

The sun begins to fade
disappearing out of sight
the colours change to midnight blue
as the day gives way to night.

The only sounds that can be heard
are the animals as they cry
the only light up high above
are the diamonds in the sky.

Still waters lie below the sky
and daylight will come soon
and all that can be seen at sea
are the shadows of the moon.

Rachael Ford

SUMMERTIME

Dew refreshing the verdant pastures,
Sun opens his eyes on a bright new day,
Silver-tinted flowing stream
Meanders along a distance away.

With eager steps I climb a nearby hill
So I can better see,
The vast panorama clearly visible to me,
Summer sights; summer sounds.

Heady perfume of dancing flowers,
Leaves that crackle like breakfast flakes,
Sunshine followed by cooling showers.
Summer sights; summer sounds.

Bees buzzing and birds singing,
Velvet wings of butterflies
Brushing past my hands,
Ice cream cooling fevered brows
Bare feet tickled by golden sands.
Summer sights; summer sounds.

Lil Bordessa

NATURE'S LITTLE THINGS

How beautiful are nature's little things,
Such as a raindrop's flashing as it clings
Onto a leaf after a shower is done
And shows its diamond colours, as the sun
Lights up its beauty, then alas, it's gone.
The tiny blue tit, nature's little clown
Pecking at nuts while he is upside down
And shows how fine his acrobatic skill,
Looks in at us from wall or windowsill.
How lovely are the little wayside flowers
That come in spring, the golden celandine
By hedge and in the ditch their little blossoms shine
Wide open to greet us in the sunny hours
As is the daisy small with red and white
These little flowers bloom for our delight,
When April comes to greet us with its showers.
The little birds, the wrens with tails cocked high,
And field mice delicate, so tiny and so shy
Are nature's small and precious dainty things.
The wren in winter's snow still flies and sings.
Oh give us open eyes that we may see
These little gems from nature's treasury,
And care for them, they come with so much love.
They're nature's little gifts from Heaven above.

Margaret B Baguley

AUTUMN RED

Autumn red,
Autumn green,
Autumn lead,
In between.

Autumn brown,
Autumn fawn,
Every town,
Every lawn.

Autumn yellow,
Autumn blue,
Autumn mellow,
Shining through.

Autumn black,
Autumn white,
Winter back,
Birds in flight.

Weeks go by,
On their way,
Waders fly,
Distant bay.

Clouds conspire
With the tide,
Every shire,
Snowflakes glide.

Sun is low,
On the line,
Freezing snow,
North winds whine.

Autumn red,
Autumn green,
Overhead,
Star is seen.

T I R

SPRING

Spring is in the air at last,
Winter's icy winds are in the past.
Sap is rising in the trees,
Small buds appearing
Will soon turn into leaves.

Early flowers now awake,
Paint pretty pictures in the park.
Birds are calling sweetly now,
Hoping to win a springtime love.
Newborn animals on the farm,
Are seeing life for the first time.

God's gift of life is freely given.
Accept this gift, and cherish it
Until it's gone . . .

Spring and nature, working hand in hand.
Let's enjoy it while we can.

M C Barnes

CHILDHOOD PLAYGROUND

Beloved land of childhood I see you in my dreams
Heather hills of purple, and wild barren scree
I recall again your whispering streams and singing waterfall
And the rise in tremulous ecstasy of the curlew's haunting call

As my thoughts retreat through mists of time the years just roll away
And I tread in childhood footsteps along your leafy winding ways
Once more I feel a gentle grasp upon my tiny hand
As I converse in little girl innocence with my imaginary friend

I hear the skylark's tumbling song on a perfumed summer morn
As it mingles with the melody of the ambling little burn
I feel the dew-fresh grass damp beneath my feet
As I ramble with my faithful friend through fields of clover sweet

I recall sullen mountain peaks and lofty crests so high
In my childhood thoughts I wondered if they reached up to the sky
I remember well the granite crags where mists forever cling
And cool shadowed boughs where thrush and blackbird sing

Mellow, mossy old stones absorbed in laughter, and conversation bright
That fuelled my child's imagination by dancing candlelight
My heart with joy remembers the warmth of a hearth fire glow
And the scent of peat and wood smoke in the evening long ago

Patient old arms would hold me, and rock me to and fro
While a lulling voice would soothe me in tones so soft and low
In fancy I see those twinkling eyes 'neath hair of silver grey
And a smile as warm as the summer sun, nearly forty years away

Those carefree days of yesteryear are gone forever more
So too, are the places and the faces I adored
Memories, bounties of treasure in the caskets of my mind
Timeless precious jewels, of a childhood that was mine

Anne Eves

RAIN

Rain
wet, washing, winter rain
soaking, crumbled grain

rain
porous brick, absorbing rain
creeping pavement, water stain

rain
dirty, puddling, pooling rain
drip, dripping, pressured strain

rain
overcast, grey-filled rain
swelling gutter, flooding drain

rain
ragged rumbling, relentless rain
stinging, driving, pounding brain

rain.

Paul Birkitt

DAFFODILS

In golden notes you sing your songs
Upon a silent sway
From frilly trumpets fine and long
Before you haste away.

All glowing in your graceful style
You spurn the winter's chill
The earth shines brighter for your smile
And shames the moonlight still.

The showy golds of your display
That bloom in clusters bright:
So fresh and clean in their array
Doth lend amazing sight.

Alas, ye haste away too soon
Beneath the rising sun,
We weep, but in your fading gloom
New birth has just begun.

Oh trumpets, fair and beautiful,
You sing your songs of spring;
So short your stay, and dutiful,
As winter casts its sting.

Diana Mudd

THE COMING OF SPRING

As warmth drifts on a gentle breeze
and buds appear on leafless trees,
it's time once more to welcome spring,
a bringer of life to everything.

The mildness soothes our cares away
and gives us hope for each new day.
No feelings of anger can we bear,
when sweet scents and sounds are in the air.

Now spirits full of optimism,
we have escaped from winter's prison,
So let us be thankful, just to be here,
at this, most special, time of year.

Tracey Lynn Birchall

WALKING HOT

Like walking on carpet
The ground is full of heat
Warm and snug
Beneath our feet
I'm glad drilling has been around
Warmth has come from the inner ground.

Michael D Bedford

THE FLAMES OF AUTUMN

Now that the blackbirds, have failed to rejoice
With their chattering charm, and twittering voice
The thrush fails to listen, as she once sat on the bough
The trees are now naked, and fail to bow

The swallows fail to fly with song
Now that summer has come, and gone
The squirrels fail to run, and play
Stocked up with nuts, through the chill of the day

The bracken has turned, from green to gold
When once, Mother Nature kept on to her hold
On the flowers, that were once bright and gleaming
But now, the flames of autumn are burning

When the swarmy mist appears, with gloom, at early dawn
Till the sun appears, and sweeps it away, at late morn
While, the leaves weep, for the loss of summer
Still, beauty is shown, through all God's nature

Like the warble of the robin's cheeky phrase
While, listening to the characteristic, notes of praise
Or perhaps an angry tick, melodious song is heard
Including the notes of a sparrow, or the rare bird

Now autumn months, is at their highest peak
The blackbirds have failed to chirp, and speak
Soon winter will meet the autumn, once again
With the boisterous winds, and dark clouds of rain.

Jean McGovern

AUTUMN

Our seeds are grown,
New ones have been sown.
In the season's twilight hours
We gaze at the last few flowers,
As we stand amongst the leaves,
Swirling in the breeze.

Clare Todd

UNSTAGED PERFECTION

The day was his to while away
Evoking distant childhood times
He crossed the ford beneath the Elms
With knapsack, rod and fishing lines

The day's perfection struck him then
Like cool lightning in the air
Stealing his second's breath away
Freezing the pass of rushing time

The beauty blossomed in his mind
Then he lay down and drank it in
And the green-grass of golden forest
Flooding his eyes to the brim

He rolled his eyes and head around
To scan the lapis lazuli sky
Above the poplars' tilting leaves
Where Dali clouds edged slowly by

Conjured a sweet dreamer's breeze
Down along the willowed stream
Feeding chubby darkling pools
Roads to the vole's watery home

Bring the dragonflies buzz
Above the distant tractor's drone
Caught in the web of summer's dream
A glimpse of nature's unstaged realm.

C D Goldsmith

THE SWAN

So deep within the forest,
The lake, so quiet and still,
Surrounded by the marshes,
Beyond the trees, I see a hill.

The steam is slowly rising,
From the water of the lake,
Surrounded by the flowers,
Silence, no sound to be made!

Slowly he appears,
From the mist that's rising high,
The mist is disappearing,
As it reaches for the sky!

The beauty and the grace,
As he glides across the marsh,
The beautiful swan, so elegant,
Nature's creatures never clash.

To capture this moment in time,
Like a vision from the past,
This beauty will remain within my heart,
And the memory forever last!

Janet Brook

A Quandary

As I weeded the church garden just the other day
On my knees pulling weeds just to throw away
I came upon a thistle, not prickly, just young
A rather nice flat star shape with a tap root one inch long.

I looked at it in wonder, perfection in design
Which made me think of God's great plan held in this hand of mine
The centre vein of each leaf ensuring drops of dew
Directed to the centre root so that the young plant grew.

Then it came into my mind, who am I to say
Which plants live and which plants die on my weeding day?
Weeds being easiest to grow maybe God likes the best
And I've been throwing them away and leaving all the rest.

Imagine when I'm dead and gone and I'm beneath the sod
Arriving at the Pearly Gate to find I'd upset God,
'God's not best pleased wi thee me lad,' St Peter he may say,
'Best do a bit of penance and try another day.'

I'm not going to give up gardening, I'm going to carry on
But I'll pray for forgiveness just in case I'm wrong
For I'm no longer certain which plants I should choose
And when my life comes to an end there's too much I could lose.

Bryan Park

SUMMER

Spring gives way to summer silently and slow,
The warm energy encourages everything to grow.
Early morns awake with a magical misty haze,
A prelude to a hot day, encouraging one to laze.

Gardens of colour with an arbour for the shade,
Where you can sip tea, or home-made lemonade.
Cattle seek the protection of large leafy trees,
And panting sheep welcome a little breeze.

Migrant birds return and start to build with zest,
The sly cuckoo lays eggs in other bird's nest.
House martins build with mud high under eaves,
Sparrows conceal their nests in the creeper leaves.

Windows are opened to clear the winter's gloom,
Enhancing the sound of birdsong into every room.
The pleasant sound of children playing from afar,
All spoilt by someone's radio, blasting from a car.

Balmy days to picnic, or eat meals out on the lawn,
Some like holidays away, where suncream is worn.
But to some, the pleasures of their gardens endure,
Not thinking of winter, but for summer ever more.

John Mitchell

JUNE

I sit once more to write a rhyme
The colour and smell of summertime.
The beauty, colour of flowers in bloom
The scent of sweet peas fills my room.
The songbirds sing their melody
For all to hear and not only me.
Nature's gently whispering its tune
This is summer, the month of June.
To see that trees stand so tall
Casting shadows at nightfall.
Hoot of the owl brings in the night
But it's not dark, it's still quite light.
Summer is a mix of colour and smells
Of baby birds hatched from shells.
Of hedgehogs, weasels, frogs and toads
And all too many killed on our roads.
I stand to listen to summer's call
To understand the beauty of it all.
What nature gives to us each day
Seasons, wildlife, that's nature's way.

Mary Long

BEWARE THE MALE

Beware the venom from his fangs
The fork that is his tongue
Do not dance to his rattle's tune
Hark not hushed hisses sung

You let him coil around your life
Then feel as he constricts
The breath he's squeezing out of you
The pain that he inflicts

Don't let his colours fool you
Nor the beauty of his grin
Stare not into his eyes
They'll mesmerise and suck you in

Observe his moves, he's fast
And slithers quietly, alert
Then as he leaves he'll shed his skin
And you're the one who's hurt.

Kim Montia

BEAUTY'S BRIGHT

Spring is the time when the world starts to wake,
singing a birth of colour it makes.
A shower of rain with a fresh smell it brings,
birds glide on soft, lukewarm winds.
Animals playing a moment it sparks,
seas start to fill with dolphins and sharks.
A lukewarm sun, defrosting the grass,
summer approaching, spring has now passed.

Summer now born where fruits and blooms flourish,
a wild world of beauty, new and well nourished.
Bumble bees busy as from flower they roam,
butterflies decorate green leafy hedgerows.
A stroll on a sunset kissed beach hand in hand,
where nothing will matter until dawn takes us home.
A cloudless sky, azure white-foamed seas,
soon the tide turns leaving autumn's gold leaves.

Autumn arrives in a gold, brown, cool shrine,
where flowers will sleep and others stay behind.
Slowly the animals to hibernate they'll seek,
as the air becomes chilled and the sun turns weak.
A carpet of leaves through wooded, lake walks,
a chorus of birds their emigration in thoughts.
Breath now lingers on frosty cool air,
as a welcome to winter upon us snow glares.

Winter now here, crisp, frost snow-capped fields,
in a child's garden a man of snow build.
Fir trees stay green with a smell of pine combs,
with holly and ivy and mistletoe.
With a song still heard from a bird way up high,
a wonder fills in beauty's eye.
Rugs now on horses, sheep warm in their coats,
warm glowing coal fires, a reflection of hopes.

A A Murphy

Garden Dreams

Now is the time for
Planting and sowing,
Tilling the soil and
Weeding then growing.

Thinking and planning
For silky green lawns,
A mower that mows
On its own 'til the dawn.

When gnomes feed the plants
When at night you do sleep,
So that roses and fuchsias
Abundantly peep.

Out in the sunlight
With flowers so bright,
Where fairies have dusted
Before it was light.

So sit in your deckchair
Believe what you see,
But shut your eyes tight
To dream dreams like me.

If you open them now
This garden will fade,
Leaving just weeds
With the dandelion maids.

Beryl Smyter

OH! PONDER AS YOU PASS THROUGH

Autumn's song is of a mellow hue
Nature dances to her tune.
Over sanguine landscapes
Fragile wind doth fly
They that have to say goodbye
Enter cool and robust breeze.

As the sun languishes lower across the sky
Soft green changes before the eye -
Lofty broad leaf, in russet and gold
Haw-fruits, rosehips to behold
Ancient hedgerow hung in heavy dew -
The spider's silver monogram.

From the moist earth in field and glade -
Amongst brittle leaf and wasted branch
The spores of fungi are given birth.
Oh! Ponder as you pass through -
Rest a while and enjoy the view
For autumn's song doth linger not long.

Sheila Johnson

A Spring Drive Near Boughton, Northants

Silver haired gardeners
hide behind hedge and thicket
sandstone towers proclaim the glory of Saint George
the travellers' dusky children
play with rusting cars
a motor show of yesteryear
leering at farmers in their superior four-wheel drives
traversing muddy fields
malnourished horses
attempt to nibble coarse grass
backpackers roam lovers' lanes
as new development
rapes the virgin soil.

Paul Wilkins

BELOW AN ENGLISH TREE

I'm blithe to know this England
She who once birthed me
Before I sleep to dream her earth?
Below her weeping tree
For yet I do not know her
Nor all she'd have me see
Would gladly leave her soil unturned
To test her archer's tree
And when I think I know her
Only then shall I be free
To mingle with her sovereign soil
Below her oaken tree
Where I know my mother England
Yet folds a berth for me
For I am of the clay she cast
Below an English tree.

M J Banasko

SUMMER AND FALL

Life's growth abundant,
drear long redundant,
green pastures flourishing.
Bounteous nourishing.
Bright summer reigns.

Sun's rays gleaming,
rain showers teeming,
trees 'n' hedges bristling,
aviaries whistling.
Serene summer maintains.

Harvesters busy reaping,
endowment's promise keeping,
greenery's change repeating,
daylight's time fleeting.
Waning autumn defers.

Falling leaves warning,
frosty fields adorning,
chill winds returning,
home fires burning.
Wise autumn prepares.

William A Mack

SECRET GARDEN

Behind the castle gate
The eye is overwhelmed
As there is a secret garden
With winds of chiming bells.

A border of pretty flowers
Are yellow, pink and blue.
The busy bees are humming and
The sun beams came shining through.

Honeysuckle climbs my bird table
That has wintered many birds
Know I am waiting for the sparrows
The sweetest song I've heard.

My path is of wooden decking
It seems upon a ship
And to my right a fountain spills
Of dreams are made of this.

Then glorious baskets of colour
Of hanging and ornamental show
A wonderful smell of fragrance
In a picture with an almighty glow.

Then as I look around my lonely garden
It welcomes nature in my peaceful place.
A lovely sight,
Where all the birds can sing.

Carole Morris

A Little Escape

A whitewashed cottage with roses and arches
Flowing pond with lilies and fish
My little garden is a birds' haven
Which has a water fountain for me to wish.

Tulips and daffodils with polyanthus
Micheaelmas daisies from my window to see
Sweet pea, lavender, snap dragon flowers
Who put them there? Yes! Just little me!

The hedges trimmed and lawn so smooth
Garden seats positioned to view
Cobble stones strewn over the path
Pink and gold with some shells, but few.

Sitting alone now reminiscing,
Of my mother and father now gone to rest
This is my escape from everyday life
My little garden is my little birds' nest.

Geraldine McMullan Doherty

THE DAY

You seek, but they cannot be found.
All the treasures that are around.
The beauty in the dawn you see,
or the wonders of the day to be.

The glory in the midday sun,
giving life to everyone.
The trees, flowers, animals too.
Everything is a part of you.

The majesty in the bloodshot sky,
leaving you to wonder why?
You do not sit and watch awhile,
all the things that make you smile.

Libi Garner

CREATIONS OF NATURE

In this lovely world
I'll take you for a spin
of creations of nature
unduly we'll begin

have you seen the seven wonders
and the simple way of life
have you seen the Leaning Tower of Pisa
what nature has done to life

if Noah had an ark
to take all the animals for free
the plants, the birds and the bees
the forest and plantations
the miracles you'd see

we'll leave it down to nature
a story will abound
God's gift to man
evolution will be found.

Margery Rayson

COLOURS IN BLOOM

Look at the blossoms in the sunlight
Making drab towns and cities ever so bright
Hanging baskets, window boxes or gardens in bloom
Every place like a painting in a room.

Baskets dangling from poles along the street
While the flowers hang over and almost meet
Mauves and blues, pinks and dark red
All cared for and watered while also fed.

Boxes on window sills, some so high
You'd think with the wind they would wither and die
But instead they look healthy as we stare
At the buildings made beautiful by those in there.

Nature with all her wonderful tricks
Those colours blend together and seem to mix
All shades and sizes in a different hue
Planted by someone who knew what to do.

Gardens too in their splendid way
Look lovely in spring or a hot summer's day
Even the wild flowers near the road
Has a scent from their blossom if truth be told.

The green of the fields and seas so blue
Golden sandy beaches and seaweed too
Hedges trimmed neatly or trees so tall
Nature all around to be admired by all.

Imelda Fitzsimons

Late Autumn

The autumn leaves are falling
With beautiful colours alluring.
The woods are silhouettes and fading
Only the robin red breast is staying.
Busy squirrels are surely stocking up well!
The snakes are curling up for the winter spell.
Seas of ripened wheat are gathered in
And Harvest Festival is to remind us to sing
And to give thanks to the dear Lord,
For the fruits of the earth
Sincerely, we must give thanks!

Sammy Michael Davis

YESTERDAY'S NEWS

Corn standing golden, apples ripe on the trees,
The lone autumn flowers, are searched out by bees.
The squirrels are hiding, the nuts as they fall,
Less are the sounds of the summer birds' calls.
Leaves once hanging green, soon colour the land,
Of browns, red and golds, like a tapestry planned.
Wonderful skies, colourful sunset hues,
Though the day's getting shorter, summer's . . . 'yesterday's news'.
Mystery often comes as darkness falls,
The mice and voles hiding, at the sound of owl calls.
So don't get all gloomy, or be sad and blue,
Take a moment to look at what surrounds you.
Enjoy all the colours, smells, sights and sounds,
The trees and hedges where fruits and berries are found.
Before long there's more changes, and leaves, trees will lose,
Harvest over, winter's nearing, then autumn's . . . 'yesterday's news'.

Rebecca Gurney

BY THE SHORE

What is it, I wonder
    That makes us feel free
When we stand on the shore
    And gaze out to sea
Maybe it's the clouds
    As they scurry on high
Or the bright summer sun
    That lights up the sky
The distant horizon
    Seems, yet, so near
The scream of the gulls
    So joyful to hear
The crash of the waves
    On the beach, so persistent
The tide coming in
    So sure, so consistent
Whatever it is
    Of this I'm quite sure
No town life for me
    I'll live by the shore.

William H Precey

NATURE'S GARDEN

There once was a garden
So beautiful, full of life and green
And everything full of splendour
It just had to be seen

Full of life and living
Nature was at its best
Where streams gently murmured
A place where you could rest

Fruits were in abundance
For nature was in care
More than enough for everything
And everything got its share

There were endless oceans
Of water clear and warm
Where life was in abundance
And schools of fish would swarm

But sadly things had started
To change and go a different way
The once green and lovely garden
Had started going into decay

But nature can renew itself
The way only nature can
Earth's garden could come alive again
But for the destruction of homosapien

The Earth could bloom again
But we must change our ways
For if we continue on this path
The Earth is numbered in its days.

Anthony Walton

NATURE AT ITS BEST

Look and see and remember this sight
Nature at its best - shining and bright
The world is a beautiful place
When God sends down his blessings and grace

After dark the first light appears
Just a glow then the sun peers
Low in the sky through the leafy trees
It's so quiet - the world is at ease

Slowly the sun climbs higher and high
The day is reborn, the night will die
The sun arises, not hidden by cloud
Bright and clear - not wearing a shroud

At dawn a new day is born
The flowers reach up, the trees and corn
The countryside takes a different hue
When the sun shines and the sky is blue.

Margaret Marston

A Day In The Life Of A Tree

Just a seed, she has no 'clothes'
A seedling with no hand, no nose
No heart or brain, just roots to grow
Forcing down her spidery 'toes'
Each root brings nourishment anew
By sucking moisture rich and true
Making ready, her magical buds
Are suspended awaiting a sign to erupt
Rain and sun reheat the earth
Awakening the 'budding birth'
Pushing upward, outward too
Releasing leaves with sticky dew
Maturing leaves give way to blooms
Attracting insects to pollen-like glue
Yellow and green, the colours entwine
Jangling like a neck-let divine
Under her branches hang flowers galore
Nectar drips sweet into pools on the floor
Jostled by breezes they dance to and fro
Upping her skirts then bowing so low
Like a dancer she's graceful, beautiful too
And the fields are her stage, the wind is her tune
Up high above as the sun nears its peak
Gaining momentum she's proud like a sheik
Soon though the winds rise and pull at her leaves
Emptying branches of acorns and seeds
Preparing for sleep as light eddy's and wanes
Out of her sanctuary animals change
Carrying acorns and nuts to their dray
To hoard for the 'night' and the coming of day
Not wanting to starve they have to be bold
Out of their warm home and into the cold

Verily this is the 'day' of a tree
Dutifully standing alone, don't you see?
Each day for her, is a whole year for us
Carry that memory - don't be in a rush!

Sue Elle

HEALING CALMNESS
*(This poem was written in response to a challenge from
Revd. Michael Chantry from Oxford, when he sent a postcard
with a very serene lakeside picture)*

Dear God, You gave such beauty,
In the sky, the sea, the lakes,
And the beauty of the hillside
In my heart much music makes.
The stillness of the water,
And the beauty of the hills,
Just calms my troubled spirit
And my life with pleasure fills

With gratitude dear Father
I come just now to You,
And thank You for such beauty
Which I really love to view;
Your wonderful provision
Of the lovely countryside,
Just makes me feel so thankful
That Your love You do not hide.

Your love for me is precious
For You make my life serene,
(Like the calmness of the lakeside)
When my life has troubled been.
I love You Heavenly Father
So forgive the doubts I feel,
For I know, despite my doubtings
That my hurt Your love did heal.

So for Your loving kindness
For Your special loving care.
I thank You, and I praise You
For such love beyond compare.

And as I view the lakeside
And the calmness there revealed,
I remember Lord with gladness
That You, my wounds have healed.

Anne Gray

BEAUTY OF THE COUNTRYSIDE

Beauty surrounds us as we make our way,
Gifts in abundance that brighten each day.
Flowers resplendent in glorious bloom -
Scented and perfect they drive away gloom.
Purple-topped mountains in powerful stance,
Vibrant perfection worth more than a glance.
Cascading waterfalls sparkling and cold -
Far more exquisite than nugget of gold.
Paintings enrapture, appeal to the eye,
Stirring emotion in baby's first cry.
Vistas of promise in fields that are green,
Paradise found in a fairytale scene.
All things of beauty enrapture the heart,
Midsummer glory when day makes its start.
Beauty in nature as white snowflakes fall,
Christmas time fantasy all can recall.
Delightful movement with birds on the wing,
Spellbound we listen as nightingales sing.
Colourful rainbows adorning the sky
Disappear quickly when rain has passed by.
Beauty, the passion for which we all crave
Found in the chapters from birth to the grave.

Glenys Moses

DREAMING OF THE DALES

A man must go where the work is
    When the wolf sleeps at the door
And my old run-down farm
    Can pay the bills no more.
But it's hard to live in the lowlands
    When you're born in the Yorkshire Dales
For here there's no far horizon
    No purple-headed hills.
No wooded slopes to please the eye
    No startled grouse; no curlew's cry
Only these noisy seagulls
    Filling a ploughman's sky.

The Fenland folk are friendly
    And full of rustic charm.
I wish I could take them with me
    Back to my bankrupt farm
Now the sun'll be slipping
    Behind dark Pen-Y-Ghent
And the dale will be sweet and calm.
    Let me stand on a limestone pavement
Or sit on a drystone wall
    Watching my 'ghostly' herd descending
To the farmyard when I call.

Jack Ellison

THE PALE MOON RISES

The pale moon rises, to great the Evening Star.
Lit by the sun, her distant groom.
His light like love, spills on her from afar.
She, Goddess Moon, the pale-faced bride.
The turner of tides, sailing the ocean skies.
A silver balloon, to dispel the gathering gloom.
Long lingers the solstice twilight,
The summer sun long lost to sight.
In the evening's fragrant, fading light.
The day now dying into the inky blackness of the night.
As one by one, the stars turn on, sun after sun after sun.
A multitude of sparkling diamonds set in a velvet cape.
As across the heavens this regal garment drapes.
A creak of crystal stars set in a midnight dream.
So sails the silver moon riding the starry skies.
Until the short night flies,
Displaced by the rising sun of June.
Now too fair Venus has risen,
The planet long called the Morning Star.
She and sister Moon linger for a little longer,
Until they both slowly fade, sun overlaid.
To leave the midsummer dawn sky unscathed.

Julia Pegg

HIGH SUMMER

Wild flowers adorn the meadow bright
Lambs are bleating, birds in flight
Carpets of bluebells beneath the trees
Scents of summer waft on the breeze.

Herb Robert growing by a drystone wall
Grasses and buttercups reaching so tall
Daisies and ragwort and lady's smock
Scabious peeping from a jagged rock.

Lady's fingers and yarrow too
Clumps of clover of purple hue
Hedgerows abundant with blossoms of May
All nature joins in perfect array.

Lyn Hunter

THANK YOU

Dear Lord thank You for Your beautiful skies,
Thank You for letting me see them with these eyes.

Thank You for the trees, so new and green,
Thank You for the rivers running smooth and clean.

Thank You for the flowers smelling so fresh,
Thank You for a light wind's breath.

Thank You for light summery rain,
Thank You for herbs to ease my pain.

Thank You for all the birds singing in tune,
Thank You for a full bright winter's moon.

Thank You for clouds drifting endlessly by,
Thank You for the mountains reaching so high.

Thank You for beaches of the whitest sand,
Thank You for cliffs so mighty and grand.

Thank You for the lakes so huge and wide,
Thank You for the changes of the tide.

Thank You for grass, full of morning dew,
Thank You Lord, for allowing Your work to shine through.

Sharon Grimer

RAMBLERS' RAP

The rambling man is a free-born soul
With his map and his boots and his walking pole.
He's out on a walk that will test his mettle
As he slashes off the top of a stinging nettle.

He stares at the top of a tree-covered hill
From a stile that was made down at Dudmaston Mill,
His senses alert to the birds' sweet choirs
As they vie for a place on the overhead wires.

The flies are a pest but he can't help that
So he flops them away with his old felt hat.
The scent of the pines is as incense rare
As the branches sway just above his hair.

A bridge 'cross a stream makes a resting place
So he scoops up some water just to cool his face.
Then one last effort and he's at the top
Of the hill that he saw when he made a stop.

The crowning glory of a day spent well
For a man with a goal and a tale to tell.
So back down a lane at a nice, steady pace
All set for the week at his working place.

John Belcher

English Countryside

Dark, silent, calm,
At peace with the world.
A precious quiet moment,
A moment out of sight.
The stillness of this summer night.
A sky so clear, with twinkling stars.
A moon that shines so bright.
The air, sweet, soft and warm
Shadows, reflections, patters, on the lawn.
The breeze is the only sound
This evening has to make.
Passing gently, softly whispering,
Rustling, through the trees,
Every leaf, plays just one note,
A symphony unique.
Insects dancing, fluttering,
In groups, above the dark oak fence.
The garden chairs are vacant,
Everyone has gone inside.
I count my blessings every night,
For I am part of English countryside.

Jill Lowe

THE WORLD IS SUCH A LOVELY PLACE

The world is such a lovely place
But no one stops to slow their pace
If only they would look
At blossomed bough and babbling brook
To watch the squirrels scampering by
To look up at the clear blue sky
Butterflies dance in the air
There's perfumed flowers everywhere
Birds singing their clear, sweet song
Fluffy clouds that drift along
The warm, gentle breeze that brushes by
Hear the low of the cows in the fields as they lie
See the young foal to its mother run
Feel the warmth on your face of the clear bright sun
Hear the children laughing as they walk home
See the old man and his dog as they walk alone
Hear the church bells ringing their clear, sweet sound
The music echoes for miles around
See the sunset in the sky
A rosy glow, another day gone by
Now the evening, comes the purple of night
The moon in its glory, the stars shining bright
Night scented jasmine perfumes the air
House lights switched on everywhere
Then comes the darkness while the world sleeps
Now through the dawn the daylight peeps
Cobwebs jewel-like with dew everywhere
The dawn chorus songs fill the air
Yes the world is such a lovely place
If everyone would slow their pace . . . and take the time to see.

Christine Corby

Summer Morn

Hail to this lovely summer morn
With its deep blue sky
Where the white clouds float slowly by
And the leaves stir in the gentle breeze
To keep us cool beneath the trees.

The silence breaks with cuckoo's call
And skylark sings above the heath
As we watch it rise and fall
Back to its nest beneath.

Hail to this summer morn
When we can sit beside the stream
As it bubbles on its way to waters new
The place where we can sit and dream
And pass an hour or two.

Yonder rooster wakens folk from sleep
We hear the sound of cattle as they graze
And bleating of the sheep
While the sun shines through the haze
To kiss the gentle rose with drops of dew.

The sound of water as it turns the mill
While back to the barn a night owl flew
Hail to this summer morn
Cottage gardens at their best
Flowers nod their heads to greet the dawn
Life is surely at its best
As this lovely day is born.

J Hewing

INSPIRED BY NATURE

As along the road I go,
The sun is shining brightly,
The breeze is gentle on my face,
The traffic going lightly.
The gardens of the houses,
As I pass them by,
Have lovely flowers, all blooming,
To enjoy the sunny sky.
Oh! How I enjoy my morning walk,
Sometimes to stop and have a talk,
To others, as they go on their way,
Out walking on this glorious day.

Ena Field

NIGHT

I stand at the window and look at the night
And the beautiful moon floods the bedroom with light.
A million stars are twinkling too
And I suddenly wondered - what would I do
Without these beauties at which to stare
And marvel at, that God put there?
Why on Earth should men tamper with rockets in space
When God's hand put the moon and the stars in place?
Cream cheese! Oh what nonsense, yet only God knows
What exactly it is that makes the moon glow,
Casting a wonderful, peaceful light
That shines through the bedroom curtains each night.
The crescent so small that then waxes and wanes
To full moon, then nothing, then starts all again.
A miraculous wonder, this ball of pure light
That God hung in place to illumine the night.
Winter and summer the moon shines for me
And I stand there in wonder thinking, 'Praise be
To the God of creation,' who with such loving care
Gave me night, moon and stars, and I thank Him in prayer,
For the peace of the night ever since time began
Miraculous making all part of His plan.
With creation there's no need to meddle and mess -
Just leave it to God for His ways are the best.
The sun and the moon - *His* created light
Which ruleth the heavens by day and by night.
Each star and each planet so brightly they shine
With a peace and serenity - godly, sublime.
In the still of the dark, as creation shines bright
I thank You dear Lord for the peace of the night.

Dot Holloway

BEAUTY OF THE BEACH

Hear the roaring of the ocean, the restless pounding of the Earth
Crying out its true devotion, to the one who gave it birth

Drink once more the taste of nature, feel it echo in your soul
Let the mighty presence touch you, heal you, soothe you,
Make you whole

Join our voices with that seascape, as we sing your melody
Endless, timeless, lost in glory, praising that great victory

Death and gloom now have no meaning, night flees at the dawn of day
Creation with your praises teeming, knows the light, the one true way

Oceans, planets, stars and heavens, sing thy praises King of Kings
Listen to the songs exploding, with their love, creation sings

When your heart gets restless, troubled and the ocean seems so wild
Remember when you're lost and aching, the sea was calmed and tamed,
My child

Walk along that peaceful seascape, find your troubled soul's release
From the world take your escape and in His arms, find your true peace.

For when your heart is aching and you find a broken wing
His touch can hear the pain there, his love can make your spirit sing

Soaring out above that ocean, worries seem so out of reach
Gazing down in awe and wonder, at the beauty of the beach

Clare M Ashton

AND AUTUMN APPROACHES

We are well into September
And autumn approaches,
Bringing cheer before December
Darkness encroaches.
The ripening splendour of the woods
Will delight our eyes,
As will the ever-changing moods
Of evening skies!
Those high, round hills, by bracken crowned
And where shy deer hide,
By Jack Frost's brush will soon be browned
On every side.
Next month the great round harvest moon
Will hang in the sky,
And the hunters' moon will shine soon thereafter,
To the ring of tavern laughter
Filling the night sky.
Meadows all silver-white with hoary dew
Will sparkle in the dawn
And Dorset lambs bring life all new
As a fresh day is born.

And four days after autumn ends
And winter comes,
Christmas into our hearts descends
And into our homes,
When we all celebrate the birth
Of baby Jesus,
Whom God our Father sent to Earth
From sin to save us!

Approaching autumn will take us
Up to Christmas tide -
And God's own dear Son will makes us
Glad at Christmas tide!

Dan Pugh

THE TREE OF LIFE

Lone trees bare-knuckled by December's chilling shock
branch skeins of blue-grey veins like an old marbled hand
in venous constriction from a tourniquet's block.
As nodding Earth brings in each vernal equinox
the knotted noose, untied, releases its taut band.

We bid goodbye to winter, our departing host
remembered only as an old unnerving ghost;
gone with him too his dreary diet of cold fare.
As spring bursts forth with lightning strokes of searing fire
the flaming charcoal grill now greets each gourmet guest.

Under a lambent aureole Earth's sleepy roll
seems to quicken; the chains of winter slacken.
Anarchic bio-rhythms open up strange schisms:
celestial heat, emanating from spring's winged feet,
fans fiery tunes displacing colder Nordic runes.

Each sunrise paints the sky with ever sharper rays
as the new season heralds longer, brighter days.
Skeletons, now armatures for curled palmate leaves,
stand upright, verdant, sporting brand-new springtime clothes,
their outstretched arms bedecked in emerald-green sleeves.

Lurking in the background that old logger, Father Time
tallies us in pages of an ever-thickening tome:
the tree of life cut down we enter that new realm
where six-winged seraphs count down our yearly rings,
with no accounting for our fancied rights and wrongs.

Life's ladder weakens, then each ageing transverse bar
gives way at last; logs roll the rapids to the flume
whose rushing waters quench the felled trees flickering flame.
But hope sounds from chill darkness; beyond its shrouding gloom
consorts of angels are inviting me to join their welcoming choir.

Norman Meadows

CAPRICIOUS AUTUMN

Autumn is in a sprightly mood,
Whipping up air to make soufflés,
Tossing the spongy pancake clouds -
Light concoctions for misty days.

He watches Bacchus tend the vines,
Putting the bloom on velvet fruit,
Dancing to music of the spheres,
Played by Pan on his seven-reed flute.

Autumn is in a playful mood,
Urging dryads to join the fun.
Boldly he strips the modest oaks,
Making them shame-faced every one.

Autumn is in a flighty mood,
Ogling cherries that blush bright red,
Pinching cherubic apple cheeks
And winking at the strawberry bed.

Autumn sits in a pool of gold,
Borrowed from summer's ample store,
But when he goes he takes the light,
Leaving shadows at winter's door.

Celia G Thomas

KILLARNEY

This place was like no other, with a surreal calm all around,
The lake was just so beautiful you could hardly hear a sound.
We reached the tiny jetty, to find the boat waiting there,
And all got seated eagerly, to take in the views everywhere.

All around us on this journey was a picture so very rare,
The mountains in every shade of green painted with such care.
The sun was shining on the lake it took on an ethereal feel,
As if just by being there all the ills of the world would heal.

We would pass by a little island whereupon was a ruin
Did someone really live there once, what was its origin?
All around was such beauty, so peaceful, so surreal,
You felt you ought to pinch yourself to see if it was real.

You could paint a thousand pictures of this piece of Ireland,
But the beauty and the serenity you will never understand
Unless to Killarney you may venture at some future time,
And experience the wonder of this place to last you a lifetime.

Jo Robinson

ENCHANTED WOOD

In this early morning wood
Birdsong seems so nice
Nature's gentle harmony
Makes peace in paradise

Every branch and treetop
The raindrops gently kiss
In this dew-filled morning
There's a pale September mist

So bathe me in the roses
Sweet
Where bluebells close their eyes
To sleep

Enchanted woods where lovers
Roam
Wrapped in beauty that's my
Home.

Marilyn Davidson

FLEET OF FOOT

Will he appear tonight,
swiftly slipping from the shadows,
black thigh boots stretching
his long sinuous legs?

A glance. He stands revealed.
A blink. There's no one there.
Is he an apparition,
a fluttering heartbeat away
staring deeply into my soul,
sensing my yearning for freedom?

But an unmistakable scent
lingers the frost-kissed air.

Anita Richards

It Is Winter

It is winter now and early sometimes
We might sit and watch the planes trace
Patterns in the sky; random lines
Against the cloudless blue. And as we face
South east the sun comes late above the hill.
Tardy in the dawn, it hardly climbs
But makes its shallow way along the rim.
Everywhere the frost all whitely shines
And sparkles in the light. And all around
The water's turned to rock. So too the ground.
Whose grass cracks crisply where our footsteps land,
And clouds of breath rise as we warm our hands.
Then even after most has melted and the day is late,
There's still a five bar frost beside the five bar gate.

Richard Stead

IN SWEET VIOLETS

In the courtyard violets blow
The soil so perfect helps them grow,
Reaching skywards to Heaven
A star's lucky like number seven.

Undercover in my vision, a crow
Feasting on dew not long ago
And the beautiful flower bed raven
In sweet violets.

Now the cluster seems to grow
And the bouquet cushion nice to show
Especially in Devon
And number eleven
Plus the blossoming in that row
In sweet violets.

Hardeep Singh-Ledder

A Summer Place

A waterfall of blue and green,
Its colours bright so crystalline,
Flowing fast, flowing swift,
Chattering, gurgling, shadows seeming to shift.

Fish swim under the surface, a sight
Of silver dappled by sunlight,
A kingfisher, a dart of blue dipping and swooping,
At the side of the water reeds drooping,

The breeze so strong, so chill, so keen,
Bending grasses, movement the unforeseen,
Rustles in the undergrowth, a squeal,
Small creatures scouting for a meal.

The landscape lush and full of colour,
A glowing mass of wild flowers,
Buttercup, daisy, cowslip, bluebell, forget-me-not,
Bathed in the sunshine, the rays so hot.

A glorious sight, a panorama,
A painting on canvas, a scene of wonder,
Gracious beauty a feeling of space,
A poet's dream, a summer place.

Elizabeth Hiddleston

Mother Nature

I think we should all stop and stare
At this world God created with such care.
Summer, autumn, winter and spring,
Oh, what joys these seasons bring!
The summer is always sunny and bright,
With the flowers all growing to a great height.
In autumn the leaves fall from the trees,
In the warmth of the light, airy breeze.
They make a carpet of brown and red,
And horse chestnuts fall upon our head.
Winter brings the snow and ice,
And perhaps the weather is not so nice,
But the trees look beautiful covered in snow,
And a walk in the woods makes our cheeks glow.
Robin redbreast hops around,
Pecking away at the hard ground.
But, wait, the frost is giving way to dew,
The grey sky is changing to a light blue.
Snowdrops and crocus buds appear.
Yes, at long last spring is here!
Pink and white blossom blooms on the trees,
Then falls gently in the warm breeze.
The birds are singing with all of their might,
Now that cold winter has taken flight.
Even the cuckoo can be heard,
Taking the nest of some poor bird.
In the fields the lambs do play,
Basking in the sunny day.
Yes, we should stand and stare,
And thank the Lord with a prayer.

Grace Harding

Delightful

Delightful are the rolling hills;
Their gullies and their winding rills,
That purl along the valleys' grades,
Or tumble down, in loud cascades,
Precipitous ravines.
Delightful too, the verdant trees,
The woods and their peripheries,
Where dwell so many living things,
And, in its glory, woodland springs
A thousand different greens.

Delightful are the open fields,
And, unto them, that nature yields;
The grasses blown by wind or breeze,
Though reminiscent of the seas,
Impart serenity.
Delightful is the briny-blue,
Both coastal and pelagic view,
Yet, deep beneath its fickle waves,
How many hapless seamen's graves?
Nay - awesome is the sea!

Delightful are the mighty fells,
From far or where the eagle dwells;
Their summits vanished in the clouds,
And fells, when twilight casts its shrouds,
Have God-like dignity!
The mother of the Earth impresses
Far greater than the eye she blesses,
And all, that in her bosom lie,
The lands, the waters, and the sky,
Surpass sublimity!

Harry Crompton-Fils

Last Breath Of Summer

The long, hot summer days are gone -
With afternoon tea on the tree-shaded lawn . . .
Robin now sings a different song
As a few leaves of gold drift lazily down . . .
And suddenly . . . it is autumn;
Mellow days of amber light . . .
Hint of frost on a still, starry night;
Bonfires scenting the fresh light breeze,
White smoke pluming through fast-thinning leaves . . .
Days of mists . . . of lashing rains,
Of howling gales and leaf-blocked drains;
Then, as if by sheer magic,
A sky of soft blue
And like a warm breath of summer,
The sun burning through . . .
Transforming a bleak world
Of drab, sombre grey,
Giving wings to the spirit
And a lift to the heart
With nature's beneficent
Gift of a day.

Elizabeth Amy Johns

MOTHER NATURE RETURNS

Where once stood green and verdant land
A building grew and flourished;
And it was here for many years
That eager minds were nourished.

This is where the blackboard reigned,
Complete with squeaky chalk;
And there's the corner where you stood
If you but dared to talk.

That's where the nature table groaned,
Weighed down in all its glory;
But now a sapling spreads its wings
And tells its own sad story.

The children came, and grew, and left,
And now there's none to follow;
Where their voices laughed and sang
The wind blows bleak and hollow.

The village school, once big and strong,
Will soon have all but vanished;
And Mother Nature has returned
To reclaim what we have banished.

Sallie Chilcott

Mountains

Reaching for the heavens with their rocky peaks and crags,
That men have tried to conquer to plant their nations' flags.
The mountains of our planet that cover almost every land,
Come rising from the oceans to tower above the desert sands.
Most of them are ancient from when planet Earth began,
Some are dead volcanoes from which molten lava ran.
Some of them are peaceful, some of them are wild,
Some roar like angry thunder, while some of them are mild.
The tallest mountain on the Earth, by the name of Maura Kea,
Isn't all upon the land, but underneath the sea.
It rises from the ocean floor where most of it will stay,
But thirteen thousand feet or more can see the light of day.
In the Himalayan mountain range, the biggest mountains lie,
They tower so high above you as they reach towards the sky.
Planet Earth just cannot have more awe inspiring sight,
Than a towering, soaring mountain top with a summit snowy white.
Whether it's to climb them or to admire them from afar,
You simply can't ignore them and their massive, awesome power.
They seem to throw a challenge down, right at the feet of man,
Come and take a closer look, climb me if you can.
And that's a challenge many people simply can't resist,
So they assemble their equipment and disappear into the mist.
Some have been successful, while some have tried and failed,
The ones who've reached the highest peaks
                                    as heroes they've been hailed.
They've answered nature's challenge and stood on top of the world,
They've stabbed their flagpoles in the ground,
                                    their banners they've unfurled.
While Mother Nature has to smile, as they think they've conquered her,
But when their footprints fade away, she will still be there.
With the glory of the mountains always to the fore,
Her wondrous rocky peaks and crags, will be there for evermore.

Alan Wilson

SUMMER HAZE

The summer haze drifts
And softly lifts
Over shingle and sand.
Through meadowland,
Sleepy hamlets, winding lanes,
Round weathervanes.
Shrouding trees
And covering leas.
Floats on to town,
Lazily down
To the city's grime,
Cheating time
With easy laze
The summer haze.

Angy Lindsay

OCTOBER

Autumn is a poignant time
With winter in the wings
But what a feast to taste and eye
The coming of it brings

Scarlet berries feed the birds
As leaves turn flame and gold
While squirrels bury hazelnuts
To store against the cold

All around in village halls
Keen gardeners show their best
And hope their giant marrows prove
To weigh the heaviest

Flamboyant dahlias all arrayed
While judges scrutinise
To choose those near perfection
That are worthy of a prize

Polished conkers on the ground
Providing childish pleasure
To use in battles with their friends
All part of nature's treasure

Dormant bulbs await their turn
As sleeping in the earth
They lie until the season comes
Regenerating birth

However stressful life becomes
When seeking peace and calm
The beauty of the natural world
Bestows a sense of balm

Sheila J Leheup

CREATION

How many times does a sparrow drink?
If you stop and watch it, it will make you think.
Have you smelt the scent of the red rose,
Growing there in sweet repose?

Hear the waves as they crash on shore,
By the sea there is so much more.
A sandy beach with pebbles and shells,
The ocean has secrets which it tells.

The various fish and all marine life,
Like painted mirror among storms and strife.
The world of nature is there to see,
Mountains and lakes for you and me.

Gaze up to the heavens especially at night,
The stars and moon glittering like silver so bright.
Early morning sun rising at dawn,
We were given senses when we were born.

Stroke the feathers on a little chick,
Soft as velvet before they grow thick.
Feel the prickles on the hedgehog's back,
Rain pouring down when you need your mac.

Watch a cow wash her newborn calf,
If you see a monkey it will make you laugh.
Trees beginning green in spring pointing so high,
A damaged swan can make you cry.

With all this beauty on the Earth,
Made by God our creator, who gave us birth.
Praise Him for all these lovely gifts,
If you take time we find our spirit lifts.

J Allen

NATURE

Nature's,
              beauty
                            cannot speak.

It holds us close within its grasp.
                      Wind, rain, fall so soft upon my face.

Like lightning flashing past.
                      The breeze you cannot touch or trace.

The rose so full of God's sweet grace,
                      The leaves that fall so gentle to the ground,

Are all a part of sweet nature's ground.

The world would be such a sad place,
                      If we lost nature's loving grace.

Iris Davey

COLOURS

Blue sky
Green grass
Black soot
Clear glass

Yellow sun
Turquoise sea
Red roses
Woodland trees

Brown earth
White snow
Orange flames
Fiery glow

Silver moon
Golden sand
Changing colours
Of the land.

Joanne G Castle

The Happy Valley

May drew me onward to a land on high,
In emerald green against a Wedgwood sky
Where clouds, like idle dreams, went drifting by.

And honeysuckle scents from long ago
Suffused the drowsing senses with their slow,
Inebriating sweetness, while the flow

Of hidden streams made music in the brain,
And echoed to the valley's soft refrain,
As if their sylvan laughter were in vain.

And how the golden wine of summer filled
My heart with singing rhapsodies, and spilled
New ecstasies on whom the spirit willed.

Sweet halcyon days I so rejoiced in, when
Shall I consume your sacraments again,
And let them vanquish me as I did then?

For now I stand with memory alone,
Regretting that for which I must atone,
And reaping vainly where no seed was sown.

S H Smith

MY GARDEN

I have a little garden all of my very own
My garden's full of treasures that I myself have sown.
There's tiny blue forget-me-nots and lavender so sweet
And in a secluded corner I have my little garden seat.
Red roses so fragrant their perfume fills the air
Busy bees and butterflies dancing without a care.
Wisteria hanging heavily against the garden wall
While lupins and hollyhocks stand graceful and so tall
Carnations and pinks with their delicious scents
An old garden fork a bit rusty and bent
When I sit in my garden I'm in complete paradise
There I can sit at leisure, watching the birds, bees and butterflies.

Hazell Dennison

Autumn Is Not The End

Autumn has arrived, supposed to be death -
Death of flowers and leaves,
When they change colour and drop off,
Leaving everything bare and bleak.

But it's only time when death is fun -
The mingling of colours,
Gold, red and green on the same tree,
At the same time.

Then they turn brown and flutter to the ground,
Forming a crunchy carpet - for the children, of course . . .
Naturally, I'm too old to go frolicking through fallen leaves!
The very idea!

Conkers and pine cones, all woody and rich
For Christmas, naked or sprayed gold or silver,
Whichever takes your fancy;
Maybe dressed up as owls or other creatures.

Soon, the trees will be bare, save for the evergreens,
Mere skeletons silhouetted against the sky.
But that's just the beginning - all the time, creating new life,
Preparing the next season of renewal.

Kathy Rawstron

HOME SWEET HOME

It's good to be back home again
To be back home amongst my friends
Remembering days when we were young
And all the things that we had done.

To sit out in the garden neat
For me this is a special treat
While sipping at our glass of wine
Minds meandering away the time.

Beyond the roses as they bloom
I see the church that I once knew
The corner shop and then the school
The pretty village where I grew.

The mountains and the lake I see
The waterfall and lots of sheep
The quarry train with all its slate
It passes by the garden gate.

The whistle blows to say hello
As on its way it has to go
The horse and cart it also comes
Delivering logs to all the homes.

The village well is also there
Used when there's a water scare
And then we take it all in turn
Fill our buckets and our urns.

The children in the caves they play
They also help bring in the hay
They play with goats and swing on trees
One of those children, that was me.

Julia Amos

IN BLUEBELLS

The bluebells came in spring, they sparkled so,
And under spreading beech, put on their show,
The bells, the leaves, the grand designer sent,
In blue and green a heavenly complement.

I've often walked the paths, walked in that sea,
Of bluebells, gently dancing there for me,
Their fragile beauty nothing can compare,
A haven for the woodland creatures there.

In nature there are moments such as these,
The honeysuckle's perfume on a breeze,
And homeward geese provide a silhouette,
Against a setting sun of gold and yet . . .

In time when summer nears and bluebells fade,
Be sure they'll come again in leafy glade,
I'll walk there, all their beauty they will bring,
In dappled light, the bluebells of the spring.

Nick Hall

Summer Storm

Through stormy skies the rapiers lashed,
Against my body hailstones dashed
While overhead the thunder crashed.
The rain cruelly hit me.

The sky above was dark as night
With oftentimes a fierce blue light;
And through that storm of noise and might
The rain cruelly hit me.

Jillian Mounter

The Worker

I watched in fascination
a busy little bee
with great deliberation
working, diligently.
Such total dedication
so wonderful to see
at times signs of frustration
buzzing, furiously!
From bloom to bloom it darted
partaking of its fill
laden, then departed
with steadfast, iron will.
Back to the nest nearby
with urgency and speed
the larva there, who lie
a rich cargo to feed.
Pollen, and the nectar sweet
within the nest well fused
creating something good to eat
and by so many used.
The fruit of such hard labour
so relished near and far
the sweetness all may savour
inside each honey jar!

Patricia Whittle

BE STILL MY HEART

Falling leaves,
Like petals,
Pass my windowpane.
Autumn colours
Yellow and gold,
Drift by
On the autumn breeze.
Clouds of silver
White and grey
Hang in the clear blue sky
And kestrel keen
With open eye
Dips for food
Unseen.
In silence
The trees whisper,
As branches sway
And shimmer.
Peace in a garden
Left to nature
And the wilds
Of the open fen.

Lyn Sandford

HAPPY MEMORIES

The morning sun is shining today,
Brightening our life as on our way
We feel uplifted for this joyous ray
Responding, smiling, dressing bright and gay.

The little sunbeams dance through the trees,
Travelling happily wherever they please,
Gleaming through windows with a pink glow,
Moving shadows, they come and go.

Summer is fading and autumn grows near,
For this wonderful sunshine, give a cheer!
A picture card sky of heavenly blue
Fluffy white clouds complete the view.

Whilst travelling around the English countryside,
Discovered God's beauty stretched far and wide,
Quiet country lanes and green shady trees,
Thatched cottages where roses nod in the breeze.

Farmers harvest their crops of corn,
Working so hard daily from early morn,
The sunshine is God's gift to all . . .
Do you have happy memories to recall?

Stella Bush-Payne

The Season Of Change

A touch of frost is in the air
And the cool wind blows everywhere
The conkers are falling from the trees
Not far behind are the turning leaves
Their colours show a stunning view
With their reds and golds a warming hue.
The stars shine brightly in the skies so clear
And the moon wears a halo hinting winter is near.

The dahlias shrivel in the dawning light
After the frost has nipped them in the quiet of night
The winter pansy may resist the chill
If only for show and the strength of will
All the gardens now have a chance to change
And without our help nature will rearrange
The lawn once so lush and green
Turns a dusty brown, no life to be seen.

The worms are burrowing far below
Leaving hills of soil where your footprints go.
The berries start appearing on the trees
The winter famine to appease
All the birds and animals alike
Will watch and wait the cold to fight
With nature's help they will survive
New life will be born and the old revive.

Sheila Storr

BUTTERFLY RIDGE

Just outside the town of Bundaberg
Off the east Australian shore
Is a high point called The Hummock
A rare beauty spot to adore

To the right of The Hummock scenery
Is a home-built wooden bridge
Leading to a wooded glade
And named, The Butterfly Ridge

Having crossed the narrow walkway
Just wide enough for one
A journey into wonderland
For a visitor has begun

Through a shaded pine-filled forest
Tropical trees with palm-type leaves
Honeysuckle shrouded bushes
Add their scent to the cooling breeze

Treading deeper through the wooded glade
An air of silence to be found
Behold, a wondrous sight appeared
Butterflies a hand's breadth wide
Descending all around

Their colours were breathtaking
As they floated through the air
Mixed colours of the rainbow
Their winged patterns did compare

Purple Emperor, Chalkhill Blue
Clouded Yellow, to name a few
Like gentle fairies they came to rest
Upon one's garment worn
Friendly, soft and delicate
Like a being newly born

While observing this creation
Thoughts might develop in the mind
That if these butterflies could speak
What message would we find?

'Come forth to view our kingdom
If *peace* be the world you seek
Butterfly Ridge will welcome all those
Who cross its hummock creek.'

Ernest Hannam

A Leaf

I watched a leaf float to the ground,
It kissed the earth without a sound,
It broke away from its mother tree,
Down to earth at last, it's free,
Through the seasons, its mother is dressed,
Washed with rain and sunshine blessed,
Host to squirrels, bees and flies,
Crows, rooks and thieving magpies,
But now its days are finally over,
Gone are the wild flowers,
And swaying fields of golden corn and lush clover,
For now is the time of snow, ice and frost,
To me my leaf is dead, buried, lost,
But come the spring sunshine,
And summer heat,
I hope, my tree, again to meet,
And wander close in grass and mud,
And look for the fruit,
Of a newborn bud.

Ted Gutridge

SPRING

It is a nice time of the year
Once again it is spring
In the morning I can hear
The sound of birds singing
And the blackbird singing a tune
The buds are growing on the trees
The flowers are in bloom
And sometimes blow in the breeze
The gardens and the countryside
Are looking nice and green
Some people like to stride
And admire the beautiful scene.

Margaret Browne

SEPTEMBER SPLENDOUR

The autumn mists are creeping through the valleys,
The forest trees have donned their russet dresses,
And low above the river's twisting alleys
The ferns are softly trailing long green tresses;
Bright in the hedges gleam the scarlet berries
Of hip and haw and rowan, bending low
They bring the birds a feast of fairy cherries,
While underneath the fat white mushrooms grow;
From branch to branch the spiders' webs are thickening
With dew-decked diamonds as the dawn's first glow
Shows how the small insect world is quickening
In every nook and cranny to and fro;
Soft grey plumes of smoke are curling
From farmhouse chimneys as the days grow cold,
A gentle breeze sets the dry leaves swirling
As one by one they shrivel and grow old;
Nature extols the splendour of September,
The rich red month that paints in colours bold
Each leaf and berry that we may remember
Its cheerful brightness in the winter's cold.

Betty McIlroy

DEVON SPRING

Curling fern in Devon bank,
Primrose set in moss;
Saffron crocus, bluebell goyle,
Swift - at Badger's Cross.

Catkins poised from springy wand -
Lambs' tails to youthful eyes;
Chaffinch stealing gelding's hair,
Peacock butterflies.

Long-tailed tits are busy now
Within their lichened hole;
Young rooks scaw in needle pine,
Lively Dartmoor foal.

Daffodils in ordered rows,
Banking tier on tier;
Rabbit warren overflows,
Chestnut chandelier.

Mayfly hatching, cluster proud,
Flashing trout on line;
Ducklings marching single file -
April pantomime.

Cuckoo, cuckoo, all the day,
Pheasant in his prime;
Fox cubs playing hide and seek,
Silver - on the lime.

Edward Fursdon

SPRING

Raining, raining, softly falling
Sweet perfumed flowers everywhere,
Bushes, trees and woodland,
Gently swaying, always there,
Birds are singing, bathing,
Building, beautiful bluebells
In a sea of blue,
How wonderful is nature's gift,
There for me and you.

Joan D Bailey

An October Day

Wild flowers growing,
In the park today.
Mistletoe, bluebell
And even Queen Anne's lace.

A strong wind blowing,
Such a cold, bleak day.
Leaves in circles twirl,
Orange, golden, green and brown,
Dying and upcurled.

A lonely squirrel sits upon a bough,
Eating an acorn held tightly in his paws.
Gusts of wind blow around him,
He runs quickly to his house.

Flocks of birds assemble,
Flying northward in the wind.
It's so cold and icy
On this October day.
People passing by say,
'Snow is on its way.'

Doreen Petherick Cox

COME AND FIND ME

Take me with you wherever you go, inside your heart and mind,
And if ever you want to reach me, sights I love you'll need to find:
A field of grass and dandelions, or poppies when the barley's low.
Hedges bursting with life in spring, birds serenading you to and fro.

Branches beginning to break into bud, blackbirds building their nests,
Glistening morning dew on the grass, the time when the earth
                                            has been blessed.
Grass growing tall towards summer, their varieties colouring the view.
Cowslips and rose bay appearing, the summer sun's warmth
                                            shining through.

Butterflies fluttering gently, miracles of beauty in flight.
Thistles and nettles to sting you, and dock plants to make it alright.
Horses munching on new grass, fields as they're turning to hay.
The farmer gathering the harvest, taking it magically away.

Trees bearing fruit in October, their leaves changing
                                            golden and brown.
Sycamore wings spinning quickly, leaves falling separately down.
The smell of the coolness of autumn, mornings when the air is so clean.
The magnificent orange of the berries, when the afternoon sun
                                            makes them gleam.

The bright, golden sunset's an example of God's infinitesimal power,
Especially the arch of a rainbow, crossing the sky in a shower.
Frost freezing branches in winter, outlining leaves on the ground.
Snow crisp and white in the moonlight, when God's love flows down
                                            all around.

Take me with you wherever you go, inside your heart or mind,
And if you ever want to reach me, you know now what to find.
These are the places to look for me, if you need me I'll be there.
Just walk in the fields and you'll see me.
I'm surrounding you everywhere.

Lorna Lea

COBWEBS AND SUNLIGHT

Have you seen threads spun by spiders
Dancing through the air with ease,
Twirling, silken, sunlit ribbons
Partnered by a playful breeze?

Seen the cobwebs hung with diamonds
Twinkle with power that enchants,
Nature's richly jewelled tiaras
To adorn her wayside plants?

Have you stood and watched the sunlight
Shimmer on a new spun thread?
Rainbows mounted upon silver
Are the paths that spiders tread.

R K Bowhill

Nature's Weatherlore

If the grass grows green in Janiveer
It will grow poor for all the year,
If Candlemas Day be fair and bright
Winter in February will have some bite,
Come March all gardeners know is handsome
A peck of dust is worth a king's ransom,
Rain on Good Friday and Easter Day
A good year for grass but poor for hay,
In May if rooks are nesting high
We shall expect a hot summer nigh,
June evenings red and mornings grey
Are the sure signs of a sunny day,
Come July see the gossamer flying
You can be sure it's good for drying,
Come August if peacocks loudly bawl
We can expect some heavy squalls,
We hope that September does blow soft
Until fruits are garnered in the loft,
Trees planted in October we all know
By Candlemas are ready to grow,
Ice in November which bears a duck
From then on its all slush and muck,
And if there are two moons in December
It will be a wet month to remember.

David A Garside

SEASCAPE

The foam-tipped waves swirl and crawl across the sunbaked sand
Leaving pools which mirror the changing moods of clouded sky.
Above, the seabirds call and hover 'ere they land
To probe and potter among the shells and pebbles where they lie.

The wheeling ocean gulls whirl around and screech
Accompanying fishing trawlers sailing into port
While frothy flowing breakers head to welcoming beach
And wily sea salts haggle over fish they've caught.

Day wears to twilight, then to advancing night
And the whole scenario takes an eventual change.
The silent moon appears again in luminous splendour bright
Casting radiant beams on waters, all within its range.

On convenient tide the small pilot boat will sail
While lighthouse beams on waters down below
And moving steadily, slowly, the small craft will prevail,
Its movements cautiously coping strenuously with the flow.

Doreen F Jackson

Nom De Fleurs

Cat's eye,
Mouse's ear,
Ox-eye daisy every year.

Old lady's slipper,
Granny's bonnet,
Lady's mantle . . .
With the sun upon it.

Snapdragon,
White bluebell,
Red hot poker hot as hell.

Dog-daisy,
Dandelion,
Love lies bleeding . . .
Multiplying.

Love-in-a-mist,
Cornflower blue,
Honesty, the whole day through.

Golden rod,
Buttercup,
Foxgloves where the bombus sup.

Poached egg plant,
Shepherd's purse,
Black-eyed Susie . . .
Nom de fleurs.

Roger Mosedale

THOUGHTS OF YESTERDAY

As a young and tender child
My memories still remain
Of those happy summer days
And the smell of gentle rain
Playing in the meadow
Paddling in the brook
Chasing after butterflies
And sit to read a book
Moments of happiness
I can still recall
Happy with our parents
To help us when we fall
My sisters and my brothers
We lived in harmony
Sharing with each other
So happy, young and free
A bond that holds us still
Through our growing years
Sharing our problems
We wipe away the tears
To comfort each other
When our days get us down
Kind words and a smile
To take away those frowns.

Meg Claybrook

NATURE'S EMBRACE

Among the trees and grass so green
Is where I want to be . . . I sigh
In summer sun and warm the air
And watch the honeybee fly by.

Lazy days and picnics
Content I am today
Longed for days since wintertime
Long may they stay.

Listen hard and you will feel
From deep within yourself
A spirit of so long ago
Of this earth and all its wealth.

Nature is the only one
To give you a gift so great
So precious it can only be
Life itself . . . so why wait?

Wynn Stone

THE RED KITES

A tractor chugged up the grassy lane.
The farmer scattered the food. The tractor chugged away.
In the air, a sense of awareness
Hung suspended.
The wary birds were waiting,
Discreetly hushed in the sidelines.

Slowly, cautiously, the red kites came into view,
With a lap, lap of wings, they circled the paddock,
Positioning the food in their minds,
But still mindful of the watching witnesses.
Shy, sky specks from above,
Swooping down, like the strokes of a brush.
Further birds flew in and joined the spiral, saturating the space
And gravitating downwards.
Rufous bodies and a flash of white wing bar,
Wingspan the height of a man.
Finely feathered and the tail divided like a hand.
With a twist of the tail, as if bound by a vortex,
One dropped and then another, a fetch of flight like a shooting star.
The crows and rooks, on the ground, were shown no mercy;
They scattered at the onslaught.
A buzzard merged with them, magnificent, but mediocre in contrast.
Talons grabbed the food. The kites ate, furtively, in flight.
From time to time, a piercing call, with a plaintive pitch,
Competed with the croaking crows.
For the afternoon, the birds stayed in view.
Dusk was falling, draining the pure light from the sky.

Then, one by one,
They vanished, eyrie height, to the Welsh hills,
Leaving the ground as bare as a battlefield.

Laura P Williams

TAKE THE TIME

My job took me to different places
Towns and cities, many new faces
All was rush, had to be on time
Or else my job was on the line,
My doctor told me, you have to slow down
My boss told me, nose to the ground.

I had a breakdown, lost everything,
Started walking about, heard the birds sing
It's something I've never had time for before,
The sun was shining, the flowers in bloom
The gentle breeze shook out their perfume,
I sat in the park, had an ice cream
I can never remember doing this kind of thing.

The children were laughing, playing with friends
They talked of the summer without any end,
I started going further, down country lanes
Watching lambs in the field, what wonderful scenes,
And I've never had time.
Majestic tall trees a hundred years old
A carpet of bluebells swaying,
You don't have to go far to see nature's work
Just open your eyes and see.

Now I have gone through all the four seasons
Richer by far than ever before,
Don't leave it too late to watch the clouds drift
And feel the warm sun on your face,
Talk to the wind as it blows through the leaves
And rainbows fill the sky.

Streams, rivers, seas and lakes, forests, woods
And fields, grasses, ferns, shrubs and bush,
Nature, it's the bee's knees.
So please just take the time to watch nature's pride
Before it's all lost to the future.

Mary Neill

CYCLING IN TURKEY

There is a peace here
Peace that comes with
The plit-plat of waves
The swish of the wind in the pines
The cricket's buzz in the jacaranda tree.

There is beauty here
Thick oil paint purple brush strokes
Cover the bougainvillea
The hibiscus glows from dark green
Hedges under the olive trees.

And the smells! Oh, the smells!
Of eucalyptus and of pine
Aromatic plants and herbs
Are underfoot, rosemary, mint,
Marjoram, soft sage and thyme.

We pause by the sea and look down.
Sometimes the water seems so clear
That even Narcissus
Could see his reflection
Accurately.

Charmian Goldwyn

Norman's Tree

I gazed at its beauty
From near and afar
Surroundings were lovely
But this was the star
Belonging to nature
Yet human in ways
I'll remember this tree
For the rest of my days
Though its branches hung down
They were cultured and smart
It was clear it belonged
To somebody's heart
Knowing this love
It repaid this way
By looking just perfect
At night and by day
In this age of concrete
It's so nice to see
The natural beauty
Of this willow tree
Nurtured by Norman
This joy to the eye
Will lift up your heart
If you're passing by.

Maureen Tooze

AUTUMN

A mass of leaves have fallen, so gently to the ground
U nderneath the dark bare trees, like a blanket all around.
T reading through the foliage, so dense this time of year
U nkempt and yet so beautiful, how nature placed them there.
M agenta, bronze, rustic brown, different shades of green,
N ow autumn is upon us, pure elegance the scene.

Betty Hattersley

A Forest Walk

That first step in the forest,
Takes your breath away,
The beauty, peace, tranquillity,
It's a good start to the day.

You walk and take in all the views,
The leaves, the colours, the trees.
The horses graze and are amused
As their foals dance around their knees.

A rustle in the darkness, brings out a herd of deer,
Silently they look around, then they disappear.
Then a flash of orange, yes, it was a fox,
Running swiftly across my path,
Down into the brush and lost.

The birds they hop from bush to bush,
Twittering different sounds.
Pecking, playing, chasing each other,
High into the sky, then down.

The heather is losing its colour now,
It's perfume no longer strong,
But the forest will replace that soon,
A renewed beauty will come along.

Golden leaves and changing greens
Will show their strength and song,
The countryside will be reborn,
With autumn coming on.

I take a breath of that fresh clean air,
Knowing I'll soon return,
To an ever changing forest,
For which I'll always yearn.

Jennifer Collins

MISTER WHISTY CLOUD

Mister Whisty Cloud
Hanging still on ground
Milky foam in sunlight
Doesn't weigh a pound

Little water droplets
Suspended in the air
Looking close around me
I can't be sure you're there

Magic mist you are to me
Despite this wordy crowd
Mysterious you'll always be
Mister Whisty Cloud.

Eric Ferris

OCTOBER IN THE GARDEN

It's time to plant the bulbs again,
The annuals are almost dead,
Jack Frost is calling frequently,
The birds come for the bread.

Heavy dew upon the lawn,
The nights are drawing in fast,
October - winter's getting near,
The long warm sunny days are past.

Trays of pansies at the ready
To fill in the empty spaces,
Brown leaves falling to the ground,
The bareness and the cold embraces.

June Melbourn

Rain, Rain, Rain

I listen to the sound of the rain whilst sitting in my car.
The sky is grey, the light is dull . . . is it like this where you are?
But as I watch as it wets the grass making it so green,
And how it leaves a trail down my window screen,
I watch the leaves as they catch each drop.
Oh my, I'm so bore! I do wish it would stop.
But then I thought, why wait until the sun?
I'm getting out of my car, I'm going to have some fun.
I'm splashing in the puddles, people look and stare,
I'm singing to myself, I haven't got a care.
I let my tongue catch the drops, I'm having so much fun,
I'm just soaking wet, I'm a kid again.
My hair is clinging to my face, oh just let it rain.

J A Easterlow

Autumn Dawn

Amber light and filtered ray
Usher in another day.
Lazy mists hug the ground,
A creeping carpet, stilling sound.

Glittering webs and sparkling dew
Refract reflections of autumnal hue.
Rusty oak and copper beech,
Forest sentinels with majestic reach.

Morning thrush sings out her song.
Solitary blackbird echoes strong,
From skeletal branches dashed with gold,
And iced with frost: crystal, cold.

Blue joins orange, red and green,
Daylight pierces shadows unseen.
Morning mists soften sharp silhouettes,
Fingering rays probe spider web nets.

Fallow deer nervously sniff the air
As a family of foxes return to their lair.
An itinerant squirrel scratches and digs,
Rustling leaves and snapping twigs.

Fluttering ash keys fall to forest floor,
Nature's confetti closing the door.
Harvest is in, now sleep draws near,
Until spring's sun rises early next year.

Colour, texture, sight and sound,
Shout God's praises from all around.
These autumn jigsaw pieces blend
Animal, plant, enemy and friend.

Stuart Wood

The Maiden Spring

She crept into the morning chill
Beneath a veil of crystal dew,
Then while the early day was still,
Polished the sky to shining blue.

She scrubbed the trees till tiny buds
Appeared like jewels, shining bright,
Then scattered gleaming primrose studs
To set the sombre woods alight.

She raked the beds and smoothed the soil
To urge the young green shoots along.
Singing throughout her pressing toil
Till waking birds joined in her song.

The sun arose and sent a ray
Of precious gold to kiss the ground,
Then Maiden Spring aroused the day
To view the changes all around.

Joy Saunders

THE DAY SHIFT

Well hung the sun on morning
Supported by tree top
A ripened fruit now ready
But only its light on ground will drop

A sunbeam spell is cast and falls
On the lucky early riser
Marinating their daybreak
Night's bad dream sanitizer

Trigger to start dawn chorus
As little hearts are warmed
Comes regular nature's clock
New daylight from grey is formed

Westward bound and slowly rising
Like a silent hot air balloon
Dictator of our daily tasks
Till replaced by silver moon.

I R Finch

BUTTERFLIES

The butterfly spreads its dewy wings
Sun-warmed, it trembles on the flower
From darkest chrysalis its glory breaks
With all the magic of mysterious power.

Who, seeing it so lovely and so gay
Remembers now the caterpillar green?
'Tis like a petal plucked from Heaven's bouquet
Soft-blown by angels down ethereal beam.

So into flight, its first sweet taste of life -
Freedom and the joy that freedom brings
Towards the purple-wanded buddleia tree
That like a magnet draws those fluttering wings.

There to find a mate upon the tree
In mad flirtatious dance to win and woo.
To open wide its wings in beautiful display
In ochre browns, in yellow and in blue.

Oh! Scrap of Heaven's glory here on Earth,
Oh! Miracle of flight and fantasy
Only God could make a gem so rare
Created with such loving artistry.

From Eden's garden came the hues
With which the master painted thy frail wings,
From paradise alone such perfection comes
A jewel slipped from off the artist's ring.

Fran Vincent

ODE TO NATURE

As a girl I lived in smoky old London town,
Where the bustle and noise brought me down.
It was as a mature woman aged nearly fifty,
That I relocated to beautiful Plymouth city.

It's a delight to live near the sea and moor,
By far the best decision I've taken, I'm sure.
I see wonderful red sunsets that glow regally,
I notice rainbows and fluffy clouds equally.

Exhilarating cliff walks along the sea coast,
With flora and fauna about which to boast.
The sunlight shimmering on the blue sea,
All this beauty to feast on - and it's all free.

Rosemary Davies

THE PEACE OF THE SNOW

She loved the snow,
welcomed its first appearance
as she would a long lost friend

watched with wonder
the graceful descent
of the beauty spots

dot on dot
flake on flake
white on white

imparting, it seemed to her
a blessing as they fell
the peace of the soft white snow to you.

Fay Smith

ALMOST ENTIRELY UNINSPIRED

I find that nature offers me very little inspiration
And it causes me some considerable consternation.
For people and products and everyday things,
Are closer to my heart, than a bird on wing.

I accept that it's a wonder and a marvel to behold,
But my mind cannot conceive for it, a story to be told.
Not river, nor ocean, nor mountaintop, nor tree,
Do anything that might endear themselves to me.

Yet offices and arguments, feelings and moods,
Fuel my every thought like some poetic food.
We live within industry, in cities of smog
And only visit nature when walking the dog.

So I offer no apology to Mater Naturelle,
I'm happy in my over-populated citadel.
Enough organic substance, of this poem I am tiring,
For you see, to me, nature is almost entirely uninspiring.

Ross Harrison

KEEP LOOKING UP
(Based on Psalm 121, 1 & 2)

We look to the hilltops and mountains
With their green or white peaks bathed in haze.
While relaxing in calm contemplation,
We find our hearts filling with praise.

Still higher we glimpse bright blue splendour
In between scudding clouds, grey and white.
We're enthralled by their fast changing patterns
Which tease in and out of our sight.

In thought we can look even higher,
None but God could such tapestry weave;
Though He's maker of all nature's wonders,
From Him deepest help we receive.

Elma Heath

Autumn

Walking through the night-filled morning air,
I'm half asleep, but fully aware.
It's so peaceful, just me alone,
Not a person in sight, to have a good moan.
Winter is near, but with autumn leaves,
I feel the cold and pull down my sleeves.
Hear them crunch beneath your feet,
The fallen leaves, all across my street.

Dan Del'ouest

ON TOP OF THE DOWNS

The essence of calm and peace one may glean,
In a man's soul reflecting a landscape serene.
What spiritual need and natural force,
Harmoniously combine on tranquillity's course.

Rippling pasture upon rolling hills.
Daisy-flecked escarpments, no satanic mills.
A river's meander through meadows alive,
The butterflies dance, the kingfishers dive.

Birdsong accompanies, gently blown trees,
Nature's own symphony, light percussion of leaves.
Dank odoured earth, crowned by sweet smelling grass,
Floral aromas upon the breeze cast.

These sensations awakened, no longer repressed
By a mind erstwhile engaged on material quest.
That burden is shed, the senses run free,
The spirit unleashed, claims equanimity.

To consider, plan, question its fate,
To search for the elements to formulate,
Balance, equilibrium, continuity seen,
In a landscape reflection a man's soul serene.

Steve Darlow

COUNTRY PEACE

Out here in the green country
We have all quiet and peace
Very few cars disturb us
Mechanical sounds must cease
It's here we hear birds singing
Doves coo and cockerels crow
Foxes bark and pheasants call
And lovely wild flowers grow
We hear the church bells ringing
Or a train go passing by
From way out in the distance
And at night, the wild geese cry
It's windy in the winter
But the view is so serene
Even if the white snowflakes
Cover up the hills of green
Then springtime is upon us
The bulbs flower once again
Birds are mating, cuckoos call
And the snow will turn to rain.

Edith Buckeridge

RAIN

Rain, running down the windowpane! Rain, falling on my head!
Rain, gushing through gutter to drain! Rain, splashing where I tread!
Rain, dripping from the trees around! Rain, trickling down my face!
Rain, saturating all the ground! Rain, soaking every place!

Remorseless rain, incessant rain! Pouring from every cloud!
A heavy and persistent strain! Interminably loud!
On the rooftops it's a-drumming! Creating such a din!
There's a problem with the plumbing! Water is getting in!

Rain, pours on the grass for hours! Rain, cleanses anything!
Rain, refreshes plants and flowers! Rain, brightens everything!
Rain, leaks in through a window crack! Rain, seeps in under doors!
Rain, penetrates and won't go back! Rain, floods the kitchen floors!

Gently, tenderly falls the rain! In light, sparkling showers!
It has a sweet and soft refrain! Recreative powers!
Hear its patter on the pavement! It's cooling down the heat!
There seems to be no abatement! Raindrops are in the street!

Some things we cannot understand! Around us and above!
I know the One who's in command! God rules in perfect love!
Floods may cause such devastation! He's never far away!
No one else can bring salvation! Upon a rainy day!

Jenny Stevens

The Countryside

Close your eyes and imagine
The countryside on a warm summer's day
You walk into your created picture
Your cares all drift away

The air is stirred by a bird
Perched on a hawthorn bush
Melodious notes exploding forth
The sweet song of the thrush

Bees are busily buzzing
Engaging flower after flower
Butterflies fluttering silently
You begin to feel God's power

You catch the glimpse of a rabbit
Crouching on the grass lush and green
The countryside is vibrant and alive
In your mind you gaze at this scene

You are in the world of nature
You picture the work of the Creator's hand
And it blends in with your troubles and cares
As part of God's mysterious plan.

Joan Magennis

GENTLE RAIN

Five years I lived, in wartime days,
    Where seasons seemed but two;
The wet and the dry, the hot and the chill -
    Spring and autumn, we scarcely knew.

A short and sudden flowering
    Which changed to months of drought;
The brief relief of heavy dews
    Before the floods were out.

There came a week of greying skies,
    Of seas no longer blue.
Home's autumn's welcome greeting us,
    Enfolding us anew.

Her gentle rain, her golden sun,
    Their benison bestow;
Friendly and strong and tolerant
    The people whom we know.

You rain clouds that may swiftly part
    Leaving your jewels behind,
May we in such gentle christening
    Your true reflection find.

Kathleen M Hatton

STORM

How still the air, how hot and still!
No sound I hear, no bird does trill.
The lowering sky in threatening mood
Piles thunder clouds o'erhead, to brood.
Far, far away, the rumble comes
A muffled beat of heavenly drums.
Then distant flash portends the power
Of beating rain in steady shower.
Storm wind bends trees like matchstick men
As thunder reverberates again.
Hearts skip a beat and wait the sight
As awesome fire sends gloom to flight
When lightning strikes from Heaven to Earth;
Making man feel of little worth
Before the strength and might of He
Who controls air and earth and sea.
Oh! Tiny mortal! Contemplate,
For never shalt thou reach the gate
The grand Creator bars to thee.
Before Him . . . even storms must flee!

E Balmain

The Sun Worshipper

Oh tiny brown speckled bird
Both far and wide your voice is heard
High in the blue you hover and sing
As in a world of your own you herald the spring
Only with strained eyes may you be seen
As your mate sits and listens from meadow green
But as the sun fades and the day is through
And the land once again is kissed with dew
You close your wings and fall from the sky
As if you had a wish to die
Then flutter, land on your feet and run
To be with your mate, till the return of the sun.

E D Bowen

VIBGYOR

The sky is awash, like a great dark curtain
And the air it is humid, of that I am certain.
One minute ago, the sun shone all around
With small fluffy clouds nearly touching the ground.

The rain, it was gentle and pattered right down
And then, of a sudden, the clouds gave a frown
Of outrage and anger, and gathered around
The white fluffy clouds, that near touched the ground.

When rain came thundering upon all around
It broke all the flowers, stood proud from the ground
And beat like a drum on the rooves high and low
The 'might of the sky' was a wonderful show.

Then all of a sudden, the sun it shone through
And darkness turned lighter, such a brilliant blue
The rainbow arrived, like an arc in the sky
And near touched the ground, a half circle, so high.

The colours were vivid, when first it came out
Violet, indigo, blue - they all seemed to shout,
'There's more colours behind us!' and here is the green,
Then yellow and orange and red, it would seem.

The colours they glowed, to the world they all show
Pure beauty and radiance, we saw it, we know
Then all of a sudden, the colours, they died,
As if all had burnt out, 'twas as if I had lied!

The rainbow it faded and passed back in the clouds
The colours, so lovely, now covered in shrouds.
And the light, it came rushing, fast, returned to the sky
No one could have made this, only God up on high.

Maureen Westood O'Hara

BRIGHT PROSPECT

I early rose and did espy
A sparkling, glittering leylandii;
Such diamonds, pure, of every hue
I wish that I might give to you.

So often are you in my mind,
Your loveliness is there enshrined.
Those precious, darling eyes, so true,
Are brighter sparkling than the dew.

The rising sun lights up my view,
Flushed pink, tinged gold, with green and blue:
A graceful swan untucks its head,
But, sweetly-blushed, you lie abed.

A gentle breeze disturbs your hair,
Your cheek may brush - for I'm not there -
And as it does your face caress,
I yearn for you and say, 'God bless.'

A world of beauty you conceal
Within your heart - and that is real!
Your loveliness dispels all gloom:
It's like the sun, that lights your room.

And though I wait a sunny while,
Until we meet, just by the style,
You are the treasure of my life
And, one day soon, shall be my wife.

Gareth Wynne Richards

POND LIFE

white water lily rooted deep
profuse alba flower peep
crowfoot leaves floating flat
with buttercup-curled cravat

over the surface upside down
waterboatman, nature's clown
pond-skaters, crickets too
as leaping frogs come into view

below, spiders spin their bubbled bell
close to red-blooded ramshorn in crimson shell
shrimp, mayfly larva for fish and fowl
deep, where hungry predators prowl

stick insects, two inches long
seek their fill 'midst a tumultuous throng
male stickleback role reversal, play
nest and nurture, whilst their females stray

mosquitoes, midges, water fleas
breed 'neath shade of willow trees
beetles, algae, microscopic lice
alder-damsel-fly entice

jungle aquatic, bacteria, insect plant
cosmopolitan fringes fascinate, enchant
rush, reed, sedge 'midst loose-strife
open ponds that teem with life

Brian Strand

HEDGEROWS IN JUNE

Now is the wild rose sprung
As green life emerges
all along the country lanes
Tall grasses line verges.

And here and there come birds
For shelter in their nests
The fluttering movement shows
Their nurtured feathered guests.

But stay; the hedgerow yields
A maze of nature's flowers
A mist of lady's lace,
Speedwell in leafy bowers.

Red campions vie with tints
Germander speedwell blue
And honeysuckle vines
Display a tender hue.

High up come summer birds
They dart and cleave the air
And way beyond the hedge
See sheep with lambs to care.

Reg James

The Wilderness

Stretching before me a vast desert of green,
Splashings of colour from an artist's brush,
Creatures concealed, never been seen,
Vegetation, dense, humid and lush.

A big cat moves on the prowl,
From the undergrowth eyes peer out,
Foreign faces contort with a scowl,
Stealthily moving, crawling about.

The sun beats down, its powerful rays
Illuminate colours within tree bark,
Secret eyes avert their gaze,
While others nestle in the dark.

The zephyr causes plants to unsettle,
Disturbing insects in the soil,
A diversity of colours and all sorts of petals,
Elsewhere ants continue with their toil.

The sand blows continually,
Moving in the dry and arid heat,
Their grains stretching from here to infinity,
Yet strangely close to the bustling street.

Two enormous trees stretch high above the ground,
Probing for water, their crusted roots
Mix in the multitude of colours and sounds,
Producing many flowers and fruits.

An umbrella of leaves busily intercepts,
As rain settles on grass like dew,
Sparkling outside as they reflect,
Readily emphasising the hue.

I'm not in the rainforest or the sub-Sahara,
It is in fact my own back garden.

Ruth Morris

THE COLOURS OF SPRINGTIME

After long days of darkness, cold winds and rain,
Nature's proclaiming that spring's here again,
For in gardens and roadsides triumphantly showing
Are snowdrops and crocuses, primroses and daffs,
Whilst down in the woods ever patiently spreading
Are oceans of bluebells all covering the ground
With the colours of springtime released and unbound.

On the branches of trees their buds are now showing,
Pastels and bronzes, bright greens and pale,
In infinite hues one's eyes to assail,
Yet changing each day as part of the link
With almond and cherry in mixed tones of pink,
Wild cherries and chestnuts all decked out in white,
Each proudly proclaiming their right to partake
In the colours of springtime's perennial remake.

Birch, hazel and willow, and a great many more
Are bursting with catkins in colours galore.
The white of the birch trunks, the brown of their twigs,
Fresh greens of new leaves transforming their sprigs.
High up in that spruce tree its flowers are all red,
And on others the new growth's beginning to spread,
The bright tips contrasting in the still cool sunlight
For the colours of springtime are indeed quite a sight.

So next time you go out look around you and see,
Wake up to the wonders, whatever they'll be,
But be quick for the colours will change every day
And you'll never again see the self-same display
For each day is different, new tones will appear,
For her palette is filled with all kinds of hues,
And the colours of springtime just part of her clues.

John Harrison

Blooming Lovely

D elightful and blue
E xceptionally true.
L ovely and lofty,
P leasing the eye,
H ue, blue as the sky,
I t transcends others.
N ectar in abundance,
I nviting the bees.
U nlike any other,
M ajestic and regal
S tately *delphiniums.*

Winsome Mary Payter

MEMORIES OF LIFE

Many places have stirred my heart
To sing the praises, tell the story,
Of nature's art in the scenery around,
Sunrise and sunsets in all their glory.

The landscape of Cumbria, waterfalls, hills,
Lakes with mountain backdrops and views,
Age old villages, rambling farms,
Ancient stone buildings, clouds, in all hues!

Wales, Snowdonia, Swallow Falls, sheep on hills,
Cottages, nestling in picturesque scene.
Devon, Cornwall, the call of the sea,
Woods full of bluebells, England's green.

Canadian Rockies, emerald lakes,
Oregon Redwoods, so stately,
Standing while thousands of years went by,
Yet looking as if planted lately!

Herds of deer, roaming wild,
Grizzly bears with a cub to protect!
Buffalo wandering in Yellowknife.
Cornwall - The Eden Project.

Birds of the air, with haunting songs,
Butterflies in the sun!
Nature is awesome, benevolent, beguiling,
Fearsome, when threatened, but always smiling!

E M Eagle

Hope

A cautionary bite in the sighing wind
    tells that winter is night
The rasp in its voice warns the world
    that autumn is passing by.
The open fields are bare and bleak -
    rime covers the shrinking earth,
Nature lies dormant beneath the sod
    preparing for the new year's birth.

Anxiously I stand and look around
    and despair at what I see.
Just emptiness - no sign of flower -
    no trace of leaf on tree,
Hoarse-throated gulls wheel endlessly
    across the lowering sky,
Echoing the shriek of the northerly gale
    bullying its angry way by.

I see flurries of feather snowflakes
    falling from on high,
Slow, like frozen bitter tears
    spilling from the leaden sky,
Encasing the iron-hard landscape
    in a cloak of virgin white,
Muffling the cries of the circling gulls
    aloft in their searching flight.

But look! There's a cheeky red robin
    perched proudly in his tree,
With his bright friendly knowing eye
    he's cheekily winking at me.
His cheerful chirp uplifts my soul,
    and as he starts to sing,
I know it will not be very long,
    before we welcome another spring.

F R Smith

Four Seasons

Take a walk in the spring
And hear the birds sing,
Rejoice all is coming alive,
Wall flowers, daffodils, bluebell and crocus,
Through the dark days they survived.

Take a walk in the summer
And smell some more flowers
Lilies, carnation and rose,
Just sit in the garden
Feel the warmth of the sun
Close your eyes for a peaceful doze.

Take a walk in the autumn,
Walk down country lanes,
The leaves turning brown, red and gold.
The blackberries ripen and apples too,
Time for a pie for me and you!

Take a walk and look up,
It's falling 'white stuff',
It's snowing, it's frosty, it's cold,
Clap your hands, stamp your feet
And to all that you greet
Say merry Christmas! The year is now old.

Take a walk and admire, it's winter,
The stars and the moon shine above,
Nature in all its glory
From the God of wonder and love.

Rachel Mary Mills

TRANSFORMATION

There's a path which leads to nowhere
At the bottom of the lane,
Ending in a patch of common ground,
Where piles of garden rubbish
Find their final resting place,
In ugly, tangled, twisted, withered mound.
Uncared for and untended,
An eyesore and a dump,
A blot upon the landscape. A disgrace.
No birds, no bees, no butterflies,
No creatures of the field,
No, nothing lived, in that benighted place.

Till nature, taking pity
On the sad, neglected spot,
Called upon her fairies and her sprites
To sprinkle it with magic and
To weave a spell or two,
Filled with joy and wonder and delight.

And there, one sunny morning,
I beheld their handiwork,
Fair as any cultivated plot.
Spangled o'er with daisies,
Dipped in dandelion gold,
With, here and there, a shy forget-me-not.
All wrapped round with poppies
And garlanded with light.
A vibrant chord in earth's sublime refrain.
A little bit of Eden, located just beyond
The path which leads to nowhere,
At the bottom of the lane.

Trica Sturgeon

COLOURFUL SKY

Early morning pale blue sky
Puffy clouds way up high
Dawn has broken, a lovely sight
Rainbow colours in the height
Turquoise, indigo, shades of gold
Look up, capture it on hold
The sky looks different every day
To be described in one's own way
A plane on early morning flight
Visible by a twinkling light
Bright daylight now at early morning
Different as it was dawning
Full of surprises is the sky
Shades and hues as days go by
Early evening the sky turns pink
Streaks of gold, more beauty I think
Dark patches with silver too
Even still some shades of blue
Not long now a crescent moon
It will be full darkness soon
The sky surely does amaze
Watching from the early morning haze.

Ethel Wakeford

THE ROSE

Flower of exquisite beauty,
Purely fashioned rose,
Reigning supreme in your glory
Basking in repose.

No flower blooming on this earth
Is half as fine as you,
No lovelier folding blossom,
When glistening with dew.

As England's queen of colour
Renowned both far and near,
You are the very essence of what
England holds most dear.

Your velvet petals pink and white,
Or red of any shade,
Exude their fragrance to the air,
Though summer soon will fade.

Rozetta Pate

Drum Rolls In The Park

Many the day has passed by
Since I first brought to eye
A fine woodpecker
Beating the bark
Now from the sycamore tree
Three gapers I see
As new life springs forth
With a squawk.
As she flits to and fro
How sturdy they grow
Since her drumbeats
First echoed the park
And there's a wonder in me
If one of those three
I will meet again
Beating the bark.

B Wardle

A Hidden Flower

Growing through the changing soil,
The sun won't always be so loyal,
Rain pattering on petals so bright,
Daylight changes into night,
Often cold surroundings chill,
Wild beasts that hunt to kill,
Looks so contempt but that's unsure,
Feelings inside mean so much more,
Unable to talk, to confide, to tell,
Bursting inside, longing to yell,
Someone listen, someone care,
Someone see what's really there.

A hidden heart a wall built strong,
Will this protect it when things go wrong?
A deep reflection yet unknown,
So afraid of being alone,
A mind of dreams, ambitions too,
With strong will power they'll all come true,
A heart that loves, a heart so close,
For all those people that matter the most,

With sunshine burning, sizzling hot,
Palisade cells protect it from rot,
The gentle breeze that cools the air,
Flourishing petals that always care,
Through the strongest of weather,
Through the glorious days,
Lives are changing in so many ways.

Rebecca Timothy

SECRETS OF THE FOREST

Down in the forest where the tall trees grow
There are many secrets that not many people know
In parts the river runs silent, dark and deep
Then bubbles along through stones and boulders quite steep
It tinkles merry sounds as on its way it goes
Splashing, gurgling and chattering as it flows
It tumbles about then around some bends
Gathers momentum as over a drop it wends
Into a pool where salmon may leap
Otters at play, beavers a dam to keep
Sun dapples the leaves, branches spring into light
With wonderful patterns, a glorious sight
Birds fly about seeking some flies
Skylarks soaring and singing on high in the skies
Soporific sounds of the busy bees
Gathering nectar, whilst in the trees,
A woodpecker drums at the bark so fast
You admire their colours as the sounds echo past
The floor of the forest so lush and green
As varied flowers grow they brighten the scene
In spring it is carpeted a magnificent blue
Intersected with daffodils and primroses a beautiful hue
You may witness some rabbits hopping at play
A buzzard drifting by looking for prey
The rustle of leaves as they dance on a breeze
You stop to admire the view, so at ease
On through to autumn, colours now change
Yellows, reds, ochres, and peach are the range
Leaves crackle and crunch underfoot as you walk
Flowers all gone now, only a bare stalk
Jack Frost pays a visit with stealth overnight
Covers all in his path with white diamonds so bright

Myriad patterns geometrical of shape
Amazement at nature, you just stand to gape
The still hush of winter when covered in snow
A wonderland to treasure, for some to know.

Marjorie Leyshon

THE NEST

A pair of loving wood pigeons built a nest in a shady tree
Their constant comings and goings were a joy to be seen
As I lay sunbathing in the shade of their home
I learned to understand their cooings by the different tones.
As the weeks went by the lovers had no rest
For by this time there were two fledglings in the nest
A busy time for father bringing food home for the chicks
And mother busy repairing the little nest with broken twigs
The chicks were growing rapidly, covered in soft grey down
Demanding food noisily with a harsh chirping sound
And I was happy to see them so, healthy, cosy and warm,
But nature can be very cruel, it brought along a storm
The freak winds were very strong, blowing everything asunder
And they lasted all night long, roaring loud as thunder
The next morning I went to have a look around
But from the tree came not one sound
For at my feet lay two dead chicks, dashed from the nest
tiny bodies lying smashed as they lay there at rest
Carefully I bury the tiny little birds
I feel so desolate and can find no words
All I can do is stand and cry
As I watch the bewildered parents circling the sky.

Christine Spall

NATURE'S BOUNTY

Gardens, peaceful retreats,
Be it parkland, meadows,
Sleepy hollows,
Stately gardens
Of mansions grand,
Even a small plot of land.
A place to be yourself,
The wonders of nature never fail
She weaves her magic
As a season follows season
Without rhyme or reason.
Perfume from blossom,
Trees - paintbox green
And Dora's garden, wonderful scene.
So enjoy the wonders
Nature weaves
In gardens and woodlands
To bring colour and beauty
All over the land,
Carefully painted, as if by hand,
Just as she planned.

Margaret Parnell

SUMMER SENSES

What summer means to me:

The rustle of leaves, the droning of bees,
Tasty cream teas, golden sands and blue seas.

Strawberries and cream, playing bowls on the green,
Deckchairs to dream, cones of ice cream.

Walks in the wood, luscious picnic food,
Mother duck with her brood, happy holiday mood.

Fluffy clouds in clear sky, gulls mewling on high,
Soft breezes that sigh, butterflies fluttering by.

Deep purple heather, hot sunny weather,
Crack of willow on leather, a soft downy feather.

Sweet scent of a flower, babbling brook's power,
Cattle which lower, the hum of lawnmower.

Distant church bells' ring. Hark! How the birds sing!
Iridescent dragonfly wing, life is so full of zing!

Soft summer rain, hiss of steam train,
Cool, shady, leafy lane, full moon on the wane.

Mist on the river's reach, fresh, warm, juicy peach,
Children on the beach, bucket and spade for each.

Village teams playing cricket, thwack of a tennis racket,
Horse racing at Ascot, chirruping of a tiny cricket.

Long, shadowy twilight, moths dancing in moonlight,
Hot air balloon in flight, owls hooting all night.

Salty tang in the air, the white scut of a hare,
all the fun of the fair, friends who really care.

Spray from a sprinkler hose, waves that tickle toes,
Velvet petals of a rose, sniffed deeply with the nose.

No one can deprive us of our senses five,
They help us to survive, and keep nature alive.

G D Furse

FROG BOG - COOL POOL

Sam met Kev, his friend
down by the drainpipe's bend
'Hi, Kev,' said Sam and waited
Kev was slow.
'Past the compost bin a hole was dug
and water gurgled in making a pond
not large, but suitable for us.'
Kev paused and Sam's eyes boggled.
'Let's go see.'

They hopped in unison to paradise -
Leafy herbage girdled a pool full two foot radius
Quaking grass leaned over cool dark water
Marsh marigold and iris bloomed by lily leaves.
Sam took the plunge then surfaced.
'It's deep with good rich mud below and stones for cover.'
Kev took a header.

Rocks circled the pool with icy caves between,
patios for sunbathing where a frog might linger
and lily pads good for a croaking singer.
Safe for spawn and tadpoles too.
Sam's thoughts wandered to a young frog he knew.
Shirl would like this -
A consortium of flats and hymeneal bliss.

Barbara Thomas

SPARE A THOUGHT

Who are you? The one who decides
Which animals live and which ones die
Leave them alone, please let them be
Let them roam wild, let them be free
You feed them up and give them a bed
In coming weeks they will be dead
It breaks my heart to hear them cry
All locked in pens as I hurry by
How would you feel if it happened to you
After six weeks when your baby is due
They take it away, it's ready for slaughter,
That could be your son, or even your daughter
Everything living on Earth has a right
To live and be free, or put up a fight
Our poor dumb animals, don't have a say
I hope it ends soon or stops one day
Farmers have families and jobs I know
But please make a living from things that you grow
You don't need to slaughter, we don't need meat
There's plenty good things on this Earth we can eat
So all give a thought for the next sheep or cow
When your wife is in labour, you're wiping her brow
Remember the feelings you had when it's born
And think of the lamb from its mother its torn
Remember the feelings when your baby cries,
You make him feel safe and wipe his eyes
Then think of the lambs as they bleat for their mums
They're cold and they're scared and their future is glum.

Wendy Meeke-Davies

RAINBOWS OF CHEER

As one walks the path of Earth's life,
May rainbows bring hope over strife,
With sunbeams shining, bring us mirth,
Renewed strength, cope on this dear Earth.
A friendly greeting, a kind smile,
Will do wonders, cheer all the while.
never fear, all is well and blest,
Beneath the dove's wings all can rest.
Life is so full of rainbows fair,
Uplifting the soul with joys rare,
May cheer, shine here with sunbeams gay,
Grater joy, thanks, all our day.
As life journeys, may kindness grow,
Warmth of cheer, ever brighter glow.
So we will walk our Earth in peace,
Our hope, faith and love never cease.

Joan Egre

BUTTERFLIES

Beauteous butterfly, butterfly,
Flutter by, flutter by.
How you flit from flower to flower
Up on high or lower,
With brilliantly coloured translucent wings
Dazzling concentric rings
Red admiral or painted lady
In sun and spots shady
See clouded yellows, peacocks too,
That dance for me and you
Once were caterpillar larvae grown
now beauty of your own
You move on south when autumn arrives
Leaving us empty skies
But what alas is your fate in store
Just pinned fast to a board.

Terry Daley

CHANGES

I look down at you, blanket on the ground,
your colours of blue and every hue.
I look down from my canopy of green,
up in this oak tree I can't be seen.
I'm sheltered from the fierce yellow glow
as I watch the birds fly by, so sultry - so slow.
At the age of eight, I watch the gate, to see the
                              farmer striding along;
on his voice is always a song.
how I love this summer scene,
all is shining, all is clean.

I look for you, blanket on the ground,
why are your colours nowhere to be found?
I no longer have my canopy of green,
the oak tree is no longer to be seen.
The yellow glow just seems to throw a paler light on all.
The birds I watched then, now don't even call.
Now my age is forty-eight
I can no longer see a gate.
No farmer sings his song;
he looked so proud, he looked so strong.
Now there's no blanket on the ground,
It's just buildings that seem to abound.

Christine Gibson

VALLEE DE MAI

In paradise
Stands a valley
Shrouded in myth
Magic and tryst
And well known
As the natural home
Of the Coco-de-Mer
The valley
Covered with trees
Of a palm unique
Of species male and female
Filled with a mysterious tale
Of romance
On a dark stormy night.

As I enter the valley
I hear
The gentle murmur
Of the stream flowing by
Rays of sun on giant trees
Make patterns of light and shade
And I wonder
If Heaven has opened its gate
Through this garden of splendour.

Suddenly
The silence is broken
And the valley is woken
By a loud whistled cry
A resonating shrill
A thrill
Even though not easily seen
Hidden in the thickness of the green
The parrot black and rare
Is still somewhere there.

Sudha Shrotria

The Seasons

Through the changing seasons, my love for you will grow.
Within the silent hush of winter, beneath its canopy of snow.
Everything is sparkling white and in the frosty air
Icicles droop like crystal teardrops from heavy laden bough.
Oak and ash, adorned in silver cobwebs,
Iridescent shafts of sunlight on the lake.
And robin sings within his icy reach.
Images to gladden any aching heart and
Create an aura of serenity and peace.

I remember you in springtime, as I watch the circling birds,
Heralding the beginning of nature's new rebirth.
A myriad of fragrant flowers, fields of golden daffodil,
Budding trees and droning bees and creaking watermill.
While endless skies aligned in harmony with rugged Mother Earth,
Carpets of nodding bluebells, the cuckoo and the swallow
Tiny lambs and rabbits skipping in and out the leafy hollow.

Summer where true love blossomed under the lilac trees,
Butterflies and bluebirds and gentle mistral breeze.
Where we picked the scarlet poppies, and walked the fields of gold
And sat beside the weeping willows when the day was growing old,
Skimming stones across the water, watching ripples and dreams unfold.
Sparks rose up from the evening campfire, like dancing fireflies,
Reflections of this rosy picture were mirrored in your dark eyes.

With falling leaves of autumn, wistful memories linger still,
As I watch the moon weave her magic, as she rises above the hill
Making dark purple shadows of evening seem comforting and still
And the only thing to break the spell is a soulful whippoorwill.
Rusty leaves rustle beneath my feet as I watch the dying sun,
Only to realise love is like ever changing seasons
And the best is yet to come.

Jilly Tynan

SUMMER

We wake to a beautiful sunrise
Birds sing a chorus at dawn
The winds caress, the earth is blest
Then surely summer is born.

Flowers in the meadow, sheep on the hill
Red poppies appear in the corn
When trees are laden with blossom
Then surely summer is born.

Rainbows arched across the sky
Dewdrops on roses each morn
Trees are dressed in their Sunday best
The surely summer is born.

When leaves are falling like raindrops
Their beauty all tattered and torn
We see mist on yonder mountain
Then surely summer has gone.

Lydia Barnett

WAY OF THE RIVER

The river was born among the mountains
In a cradle of ice and snow
From frozen peaks to distant sea
There will be a long way to go . . .

By flowing across borders of countries,
Extensive plains and lively towns
It touches the lives of people
And shares with them their ups and downs.

Then enhanced by scented forestry air
And that of lands of morning dew
It will pass sites of history
Either ancient - or fairly new.

But fates of some places are sad:
Wars and turmoil by the day,
Blood and tears mingle with waves
And together they flow away . . .

Legends will also be flowing with them
And tales of a region's past
By then the river grows mighty
And runs on its course very fast.

A cheerful sight when busy with boats
Of so many types - big and small,
Yet - sometimes I can't help but ask:
Is it hard to carry this all . . . ?

But the river rolls on without a word
It goes where it most wants to be,
To unload and come to a rest
In the soothing depths of the sea.

Anthony Grimes

GLOBAL DESTRUCTION

The rainforests once covered the Earth
just grew and grew for all its worth
all sorts of creatures lived there in peace
utilising bushes, trees, filling every niche,
a variety of species, animals and plants
rare flowers, orang-utang, to billions of ants,
to name but a few, this was home to them all
then along came man, and man had a ball,
chopped at the trees, threw rubbish everywhere
released harmful gases into the air,
hunted and killed, destroyed all he could find
just laughing it off, with never no mind,
millions of hectares are burnt every year,
leaving creatures and man, living in fear,
burning fossil fuels, does not help at all
but talking to man, is like talking to the wall,
with the rain falling on barren land
causing mud slides that bury homes, animals and man,
killing all plants for farm animals to graze
fills me with anger, fills me with rage,
all this destruction to satisfy man's needs
will be the death of this Earth, for the sake of greed.

D Richards

OUR PLANET EARTH

The eyes behold the wonders of the Earth
The mind assesses what it's worth.
No treasures here to have and hold
No value to mankind unless it can be sold.

The grasping hands want more and more
They will strip the Earth down to its core.
When no beauty then remains
And nought is left but vast and empty plains
Hills stripped bare of shrubs and trees
What will we do when this is all the eye perceives?

When I see the moon at night on high
I look with sorrow and I want to cry
Let's stop before the Earth becomes the same
an empty shell - a symbol to man's shame.

D Adams

A Springtime Flower

It starts off as a seed,
That's planted in the ground.
It needs the warmth and sunshine,
And the air that's all around.
It slowly starts to germinate,
Up pops a tiny shoot.
And down below the earth,
There grows a tiny root.
The shoot grow up towards the sky,
To form a great big stem.
Leaves sprout out, as do buds,
For flowers to grow from them.
The plant keeps on growing,
In the middle of the April shower.
the bud slowly opens out,
Into a beautiful yellow sunflower.

Mrinalini Dey

FLUOXOTINE DREAM

Roaming night bear, vivacious scheme,
Gardens savage, wolverine.
Dripping foxgloves, poison openings
Creeping forward, leathery folds,
Burning filthy marigolds.
Days' eye smiling, pulling, struggling,
Sucking up the stinking ladies,
Grabbing at their swollen babies.
Fork tongue lapping, fur-line twisted,
Nightshade fade not resisted.
Turning, falling, mothy corners,
Webbed trees and crawling mourners.
Rotted whispers feathered tightly,
Squinting night bright, blowing lightly,
Spidery dangling tangling slumber,
Spiny tree snake lying under
Muddy loathing, blind betrothing,
Stealing limy lizard scales,
Scraping with its teeth and nails,
Lulling you to false abetting,
Lupine faking not regretting.
Violet snubs you, Lily loves you,
Blooded poppies seeping sleeping,
Leave me from the bushes peeping,
Collecting up and quietly keeping,
Clockwork dandy lion heads
And p*****g in their flower beds.
Dancing drazel fly in fury,
High above the sky is stormy,
Wrap me in your lathered wings,
Save me from fly dragon stings.

Dawn Gillespie

SUMMER'S EVE

Sun going down in a cherry pink sky.
Soon a multitude of stars will shine on
Cotton wool clouds drifting aimlessly by,
A landscape transformed with the daylight gone.

River Severn in the valley below.
Waterfowl departing on evening flight
After foraging in its gentle flow,
They will seek a safe haven for the night.

From the river bank, fragrance of balsam.
Air heavy with the scent of new mown hay.
In the distance the laughter of children,
The perfect ending of a summer's day.

Les Davey

THE AUTUMN OF ME

A talent passing,
The mind still quick, the body slow to react.
The acorns of courage grow fat with age,
Tomorrow is only winter, today is autumn.
Enjoy the freshness of a raw clear morning,
Savour the short warmth of an afternoon.
Watch the leaves slowly turn to a fatal brown,
The last heat of summer clings hopelessly,
To fragile flowers blooming.
Tonight the chill will creep closer to the back door,
Guard your warmth, precious as life.
There is a tranquillity of autumn,
The calm after the blaze of molten summer.
A peaceful reflection beyond the breaking year.

Ian Fisher

ANCHOR BOOKS SUBMISSIONS INVITED
SOMETHING FOR EVERYONE

ANCHOR BOOKS GEN - Any subject, light-hearted clean fun, nothing unprintable please.

THE OPPOSITE SEX - Have your say on the opposite gender. Do they drive you mad or can we co-exist in harmony?

THE NATURAL WORLD - Are we destroying the world around us? What should we do to preserve the beauty and the future of our planet - you decide!

All poems no longer than 30 lines.
Always welcome! No fee!
Plus cash prizes to be won!

Mark your envelope (eg *The Natural World*)
And send to:
Anchor Books
Remus House, Coltsfoot Drive
Peterborough, PE2 9JX

OVER £10,000 IN POETRY PRIZES TO BE WON!

Send an SAE for details on our latest competition!